EMOTIONAL ME

Self-Discovery, Healing, and Strength Through Faith

Kirklin Cross Jr.

Copyright © 2024 Kirklin Cross Jr.

All rights reserved. No portion of this book may be reproduced, stored, in a retrieval system, or transmitted in any form or by any means, electronic, mechanical, photocopy, recording, or otherwise, without written permission from the author. Brief quotations may be used in literary reviews.

Unless otherwise noted, Scripture quotations without version markings are taken from THE HOLY BIBLE KING JAMES VERSION. Public domain.

Scripture quotations marked (NLT) are taken from THE HOLY BIBLE, NEW LIVING TRANSLATION,
© 1996, 2004, 2007 by Tyndale House
Foundation. Used by permission. All rights reserved.

Scripture quotations marked (MSG) are taken from THE MESSAGE BIBLE, © 1993, 1994, 1994, 1996,
2000, 200, 2002 by NavPress Publishing Group.

Scripture quotations marked (NIV) are taken from THE HOLY BIBLE, NEW INTERNATIONAL VERSION®, NIV®.
© 1973, 1978, 1984, 2011 by Biblica, Inc. TM Used by permission of Zondervan. All rights reserved worldwide.

Published By: Judiyah Publishing Company
Cover Art Design By: Kirklin Cross Jr.
Edited by: Shana Washington – shanaspeakslife.com

ISBN: 978-1-7374135--3-0

Reach Us Online:
Activate Int'l Ministries - aimtx.us
Truth Church - activatetruth.org
Cleburne, Texas

DEDICATION

To my amazing wife, Ikisha, whose love and support have been my constant source of strength. Your faith, grace, and dedication inspire me every day. Thank you for being my partner in life and in this journey.

To my children, Will, Aniyah, Daelyn, J'Ohnnye, and Kellan, who fill my life with joy, laughter, and purpose. Your curiosity and wonder remind me to never stop dreaming and growing.

To my parents, Kirklin and Peggy, whose wisdom, sacrifices, and unwavering belief in me laid the foundation for everything I am today. Your love has been my anchor.

And to my seven siblings, my lifelong companions in both challenges and triumphs. Thank you for your unwavering support, love, and laughter.

I love you all.

CONTENTS

INTRODUCTION 3

EMOTIONAL ME 6

THE WARFARE OF EMOTIONS 24

WOUNDS AND SCARS 46

GET UP 64

WONDERFUL COUNSELOR 86

EMOTIONAL TRIGGERS 104

LOVE: THE ROOT OF HEALTHY EMOTIONS 132

SUPPRESSION, CAVES, SELF-MEDICATION & SILENCE 151

THINK HAPPY THOUGHTS 170

EMOTIONAL ME CHECK-IN: HOW ARE YOU FEELING? 186

CONTINUE YOUR JOURNEY WITH EMOTIONAL ME 190

INTRODUCTION

Welcome to this journey! As you read through these pages, I believe God is going to do a transformative work in your life. This book has been stirring in my spirit for some time, but the clarity of direction came recently through a conversation with a sister in Christ. Since then, the Lord has continually impressed on my heart the topic of emotions—a subject we often overlook or sideline in the body of Christ.

In truth, the church has sometimes struggled to teach believers how to approach matters of the soul from a kingdom perspective. We live in physical bodies that house a divine spirit, and these two parts can create internal conflict if not brought into harmony. As the apostle Paul said, there's a "war within our members" (Romans 7:23), and to experience peace, we must bring our bodies, souls, and spirits into alignment under the guidance of the Holy Spirit. This process, a journey toward self-mastery, requires us to address our emotions, mind, and will in a way that honors God's kingdom principles.

Our spirit originates from God, yet our soul—comprised of our mind, will, and emotions—joins with it in this earthly life. God knew us before we were formed; He predestined our lives with purpose and design. However, living out that purpose involves navigating our emotions within the boundaries of the Spirit. Self-control, as described in Galatians 5:22-23, is one of the fruits of the Spirit and is central to walking in alignment with God's will. Emotions, then, are healthy and life-giving when expressed under the filter of the Spirit's fruit.

True self-control, defined as managing our emotions, desires, and actions, is more than just willpower; its willpower surrendered to God. This means allowing the Holy Spirit to shape and guide our responses, enabling us to live out God's purpose with balance, peace, and divine wisdom.

Let's take this journey together, exploring how we can align our souls under the guidance of the Holy Spirit and learn to live fully in Christ.

OPENING PRAYER

Heavenly Father, I thank You that You are God, and You are God all by Yourself. You have called us to a lifestyle of submission and obedience to Your principles. As we discuss this topic, Emotional Me: Self-Discovery, Healing, and Strength Through Faith, I pray that someone reading this will experience a breakthrough and gain practical insights on how to apply Your Word to their emotions. I pray they will be empowered to step off the emotional rollercoaster and live life according to Your will, Father God. I thank You, Father, that there will be breakthroughs from trauma, hurts, pains, and past experiences. Someone who has been living a life of emotional distress will find freedom through these experiences. Father, You have called us to a lifestyle of self-control and contentment. I thank You that we will respond with You in mind, not our emotions. Lord, I thank You that we will develop a healthy perspective of the emotions we're meant to feel. But even in our emotions, Your principles must take priority in our lives. You have shown us through Your Word that we can be angry and not sin. Father, help us embrace that realm of self-control, where we can feel anger but not allow it to manifest or mature into sin, which separates us from You. I pray that when we feel sorrow, we won't let it manifest into sinful mindsets that distance us from You. We can feel sadness, Father God, but we won't allow it to mature into something evil that causes us to sin and separate from You. Even now, I sense something breaking, and someone just needed to hear it put this way: sadness doesn't have to become depression. Sadness doesn't have to turn into anxiety or grow into anything else. Anger doesn't have to become rage. Father, we thank You that You will have Your way throughout this book, bringing freedom and liberty from unhealthy emotions, making them no longer our portion. In Jesus' name, Amen.

Chapter One

EMOTIONAL ME

We have many types of emotions, and Satan uses them to ruin our lives daily to the point where we make decisions based on whether we're happy, angry, sad, bored or frustrated. We even choose activities and hobbies based on the emotions that they incite. When we come into a healthy understanding of our emotions, it can help us navigate life with a greater ease and stability. So, we must learn the difference between healthy and unhealthy emotions. Jesus even had experiences with His emotions in the bible. In Matthew chapter 26, Matthew tells us his account of Jesus having an emotional moment. In the moment Jesus says, "My soul is crushed with grief to the point of death. Stay here and keep watch with me." He went on a little farther, and bowed with his face to the ground, praying, "My father, if it is possible, let this cup of suffering be taken away from me. Yet I want your will to be done, not mine." Then he returned to the disciples and found him asleep. He said Peter, "Couldn't you watch with me even one hour? Keep watch and pray, so that you will not give into temptation. For the spirit is willing but the body is weak." Then Jesus left him a second time and prayed, "My father, if this cup cannot be taken away, unless I drink it, your will be done" (Matthew 26:38-42 NLT).

We see here Jesus having an emotional moment. He is asking the disciples to come with him to pray because he knows that the time of his death is near. He's suffering with grief in his soul and he's having all of these emotions arouse. He understands in the word that one can put away 1000 and two can put away 10,000. So, he's trying to get the disciples to get on the battlefield with him, because he's having this emotional attack in this hour. Life, as he knows it is about to change in a greater way for him. So, he called on his prayer warriors, the ones he's equipped to pray, the ones who were supposed to understand that they're called to be watchman. He told Peter from the beginning of time to follow me, and I'll make you a fisher of men. Peter has been with Jesus awhile at this point and already knows that he's being discipled. Jesus is training and equipping him to be Kingdom minded.

Jesus is like man, y'all need to understand I'm feeling this grief in my soul. My mind will and emotions are acting up. I'm all over the place. I can't think right, I'm trying to make sure I can make the right decision because I know I got to choose to get up on that cross when it is time. But Lord still the thought of it. Have you ever had anything happen in your life where you were like, Lord, still the thought of it? The Lord said, "My soul is crushed, and it is filled with grief, to the point of death" (Matthew 26:38 NLT). He's telling the disciples to stay, keep watch with Him, and pray with him.

He went out a little farther and bowed with his face to the ground. He got down into a low place, praying, "My father!" Jesus let us know that he didn't want God the Supreme Being, he wanted daddy in this moment. He is signifying here that he needed the nurturing nature of God the father. He needed the guidance that only a father brings. A father gives you identity; he points direction to you. He was basically saying, I need that part of you God. I need you to give me wisdom. I need the God that can help me focus.

> Will you remember him as father?

You may have forgotten him as Father because you're too busy. At times you only see him as the God who's going to give you something. You see him as the God you can beg to. The God that you are waiting on for your spouse, prosperity, and other materialistic things that are not eternal. God at times is only viewed as an answer to our problems, and we forget that he's Father. He is daddy. Will you remember him as Father? See you can go to daddy and sit on his lap. You can look at daddy and say, pop I just need insight. I need understanding, that only comes from you. See I call my biological father and our heavenly Father by the same name, Pop. I say pop I need you. You don't just go around calling just anybody Daddy or Father. When you truly know God as Father, you know he takes care of everything else anyway, because he's already done it time and time again.

The Father represents a level of trust with him. You're not just calling somebody who didn't take the time to raise you up and guide you, Father. You don't give them such an intimate definition. You don't call anyone who hasn't put in the time, that you haven't seen model what a father looks like, daddy. He said, Daddy, you already know how I feel. I've even told the disciples. But if it's possible, if you will, because I know it's up to you because you gave me this assignment, please take this cup from me. Getting up on the cross was furthest from his mind in that moment. Jesus didn't want to do this. Have you ever felt like telling Daddy, I don't want to do this?

Sometimes you get to a place where you just have to be real with yourself and God. Sometimes it's hard to verbalize how you feel to others when you are on an emotional roller coaster. It's hard to verbalize how you feel to trusted voices especially anyone who is on the same roller coaster ride as you and don't have the capacity to pull you up because they are always there. You can't depend on people to pull you up who are always down. Jesus identifying with God as Father helps us also see that Jesus took his issue to someone who is mature enough to handle what he was dealing with.

Too often people bring their problems to people who the same or more problems than them. Now you over here got Charles Manson and Ted Bundy trying to help you figure out your problems. You got Jack the Ripper trying to be a psychologist to you. Matthew is letting us know that Jesus took the issue to the Father. You know, you see all of that ratchet TV where a whole bunch of emotional, traumatized, and distressed people are trying to stir up more trauma through more emotion and that's what the world calls entertainment. People have an argument, and you find that funny. It's making them money because the world finds people in their emotion funny and amusing. So, they build their ratings on your ability to connect emotionally with unhealthy emotionally distressed people. I bet you never looked at it like that, have you?

So, they use emotionally dysfunctional people to connect with your emotional dysfunction and build ratings to make money. And now you record it, so you don't miss it while you're at work. You don't realize you sow all that same stuff into your spirit. When we put all of that in our temple, we then wonder why you and your husband or wife are always fussing. Then you and your kids can't get along because you put all that discourse in your temple. You let the kid put it in their temple. It's just reality tv, you say. No, it's a demonic spirit that is creating warfare through what you take in on your devices. That's why would monitor our kids' phones because it's too much. See as Father, I must make the mature decision for them. I don't care how they feel. They're not mature enough to handle these devices. It's so much attached to those things.

There's so much attached to other people. But Jesus takes his stuff to the Father, and you must be mature enough to take it to your daddy too. He says let this cup of suffering be taken away from me. The cup represents a measurement and all of us feel in measurements. That's why some days you'll say, I'm feeling a little better, today is worse than yesterday, or today is much better and define ourselves by the measurements of emotions we're experiencing. Jesus is measuring how he feels and he's saying this cup of suffering is so much that he needs God to take it away from him. Have you ever had a day that's just been too much? You just need God to take it. We want to rewind our morning, go back to bed, close our eyes, and just reenact waking up again because it's already too much.

There was a season in my life I was so tired because we went from conference to burying my grandmother and so many other things. We were just going and going. I just pushed myself between family, work, and ministry. It was so bad one day; I came home from work and my wife looked at me and said, so you were at work all day with your shirt inside out and didn't notice? I just looked down and thought, Wow I was in such an emotional state that I didn't realize I was at work all day with my shirt on inside out. Another day, I needed to take something to the post office. While I was waiting in line I looked down and noticed I had on two different brands and colors of shoes. One was black and one was white. I promise you I was standing in that line wishing I could tuck my feet in my pants. Like this would have been a good day to have some bell bottoms to cover them up. These things will happen to you when you allow your emotions to cloud your thinking and forget to align your mind to a kingdom way of thinking.

Here is a nugget: Jesus acknowledged how he was feeling. He took how he was feeling to someone else and acknowledges that he had an intimate relationship with God and was mature enough to conform to God's will over his own. He loved God enough to make the right decision. He's real enough with himself to say nevertheless, although I don't want to do this, not my will, but your will be done. These are components we need to embrace when we're having an emotional moment. Please hear me, this situation is extreme. He knows he is about to die. So, at a base level we need to be able to bring it straight under subjection. We can acknowledge it, but we also need to choose his will be done. I'm laying a foundation because remember our emotions come in measurements. Some days are worse than others. And on the days that aren't as bad, you should be able to manage them yourself. You should be able to maintain them within yourself. But if you're having a day like Jesus, you need to be strong enough and bold enough to realize that you can't do this in your own strength.

When you petition others to pray with you, it should be because you need reinforcements, not when you've given up because we must be in agreement. Two can't walk or pray together unless they agree. So, lets pray together, but don't give up on yourself. We have this false expectation that people should be more committed to us than we are to ourselves. I was counselling someone regarding their marriage, and he would come to me for prayer. One day I stopped and corrected him in that moment. See I kept praying but he wouldn't come into agreement and change. So, one day, I finally told him, why should I be more committed to your family than you?

As a leader, I'm mandated to love you and be there for you. But in wisdom, the Bible also says, "Don't cast your pearls on swine" (See Matthew 7:6 NLT). So, if someone takes your counsel, doesn't do the self-work and choose the same emotional state, there must be accountability. So, the question to ask yourself is, when we you seek counsel or pray, are you doing the internal work afterwards? Or are you taking the counsel and allowing your emotions to have more priority, thus choosing to stay in the same mental place? No one should be fighting for your healing alone. Both parties should be on the battlefield. We should both be picking up our slings like David. We must stop having the false expectation that every friend, family member, counselor or minister should have more responsibility for our own emotions than ourselves. Only we and God have the real power to change how we process our emotions. We have to meet each other halfway so that we stop repeating the same emotional dysfunction. In that moment Jesus couldn't get the disciples to pray and so what should have been a corporate prayer moment turned into a moment of correction in love.

While Jesus was praying, he realized Peter fell asleep. What do you do when the ones that you have petitioned to pray with you, sleep on you? What do you do when the ones you have petitioned to pray for you are silent? When he returned to the disciples and found them asleep, he said to Peter, couldn't you watch with me even one hour? Now the grief is turned to anger and frustration because the ones he thought he could trust took a nap when they were supposed to be praying. We call our people to prayer often because it's our mandate to build a house of prayer. I believe every believer should also build a house of prayer within themselves. So, we call our people to prayer to stir them up and teach them how to pray.

Believers shouldn't settle for praying carnal prayers like, dear Father God, thank you for this day. I thank you for my potato chips and my sandwich amen. Instead, we teach them how to press in and discern spirits operating in their lives and call out demonic forces trying to manifest in their children. We teach them how to tap into things going on in their regions. We teach them how to say thus saith the Lord and decree and declare a thing and call it forward. We teach them how to understand their anointing because it's the anointing that breaks yokes, not a memorized carnal prayer and nor is begging. Believers need to pray until their intimacy with God provokes the kingdom to manifest on earth as it is in heaven.

So, Jesus said, look, I'm trying to stay focused on my assignment, can you partner with me in prayer? What do you do when you call the people to serve everyone has excuses? Well God knows that too. Jesus wasn't feeling good when he had nails in his hands and took all those slashes when they whipped him all night long. He wasn't feeling good on the cross either, but he still was bold enough to break through and say, Father, forgive them, but we make excuses why we can't pray. How dishonorable to God is that? We shut down when we have a moment forgetting that God is in control and has the power to heal. Then Jesus told the disciples to keep watching and praying so that they would not fall into temptation. He said if you won't break through what you feel in your flesh, it's going to grow into a deeper temptation to yield to your flesh, your emotions, and cause things to manifest into something that you can't handle. The bible says, "Then after desire has conceived, it gives birth to sin; and sin when it's full grown gives birth to death" (James 1:15 NIV).

He's talking about a realm of your mind, will, and emotions manifesting from a thought into an action which then causes separation. In essence, he's saying stop acting like children and grow up. You couldn't watch for one hour, you're in your grown but want people to pacify you. You can't pray with me one hour? When we can't pray, we open the door to fall into temptation. We go back to struggling in areas like lusts because you didn't pray, because you didn't spend time with the Father. Now everything is out of whack. We then embrace a level of temptations that cause us to move by our emotions. We become stuck for the rest of the day, week, month, year, processing out thoughts through our emotional lens. Jesus knew what would happen if the disciples were tempted.

He tells them to stay alert because he understands how the flesh and the spirit works. The spirit is willing, but the body is weak. We have to stop pretending like we've changed and just be real enough to say, I'm still struggling. This person I know was pretending like everything was good and the whole time I was spiritually seeing skeleton bones. The Lord spoke to me and said, malnourished meaning, they hadn't been in the word like they should and there were skeletons in the closet. In essence, still hiding stuff. You see, Jesus is always sitting here, he's always making things known. I know what's going to happen with this, because I understand how the body works, and the spirit works. I need you to understand that the spirit is always willing. I'm going to say that again. The spirit, God's Spirit is always willing. He's always willing to be and do what he needs to for you. He's always ready and willing to do what's necessary for you, but because he's God, he's not going to force you. He's going to allow you the opportunity to make a choice, either your flesh, or the spirit.

Your flesh is weak because it's born into a sinful nature. Paul even tells us in Romans 8, that the spirit and the flesh is enmity against one another. We always say enmity is just separate. But when you look deeper into the word enmity, you'll find that it really means hate. So, your spirit hates your flesh, and your flesh hates your spirit, which means they don't want to be together. So, your flesh is weak, because it's the part of you that's designed to not want the things of God. That's why sin is so easy. Because it's guided by sin nature. It hates having to serve. It hates having to study the Word. It hates having to pray when you just want to be pacified. It hates having to be mature when you just want somebody to coddle you and tell you it's going to be alright. It hates standing up and being bold like David did with Goliath. It would rather embrace lust because you are lonely. The flesh would rather do anything but what God wants it to do. Here's the thing. While the body is weak the hidden gem here is that your spirit nature is always willing. Did you know that your flesh and spirit operate off the same frequencies, faith and fear? I say it like that to make a point, God and the devil both operate on the same frequency called faith. You must believe in one or the other and what they offer for it to manifest in your life. For example, with Satan you must believe the lies he is feeding you like you're not healed from the trauma. You must believe that you are nobody, believe in self-condemnation. You must believe that even though your abuser has moved on, he's still looking through a window at you. In like manner with God, you must believe that where the spirit of the Lord is there is liberty.

You must believe when the word says, "That God so loved the world that he gave his only begotten son that whosoever will believe in him will not perish but will have everlasting life" (John 3:16 KJV). You must believe that if you're in Christ you become a new creature, old things have passed away, behold all things have become new (2 Corinthians 5:17 NLT). You must believe that you can't do it on your own. You must believe that you will be married. You must believe, period. So, are you going to believe in the spirit that's willing to do holy things or are you going to believe in the flesh that's willing to do carnal things? You must believe it's okay to cuss them out or you must believe that a wise man says nothing. Jesus left Peter a second time and prayed, my father if this cup cannot be taken away unless I drank it, your will be done. So even when I didn't feel like this thing was lifted, I learned to still walk it out. Can you walk out how you feel without allowing it to go to extreme places when God doesn't lift it? Sometimes it's just what you need to get you to where you're going.

What if God says no this is my will being done? What if the sorrow that Jesus was experiencing was another reenactment of Jesus feeling the sorrow that God feels for his people? This is the very reason why he sent Jesus to the cross. This in a way parallels to how God felt when he sent Hosea to marry the harlot so he would know how God felt before he released God's word to the people. So, the cross was his assignment. He didn't forget that assignment was to save other people. He got on the cross and said, today son you'll dine with me in paradise. He got on the cross and said, "Father, forgive them for they know not what they do" (Luke 23:34 NLT). He overcame his sorrow so he could fulfill the work of the cross. He knew he still had an assignment to complete. Some of you are going through certain things because it's just a part of your assignment. Some of you are being tugged on right now to mature from that place of emotional trauma because it's part of your assignment and your mandate to bring others out of the same place. But how can you if you don't have the tools? The word emotional is defined as characteristics or expressions of emotion, readily or excessively affected by emotion, cost, determined or actuated by an emotion rather than reason. So, you go on this joyride of emotion because you allow whatever experience to impact your life and move you into a realm called emotion rather than reason.

Something happens and you emotionally can't think now. That's what emotions will do. When you don't have a measure of self-control you won't be able to think or as the definition says, reason. Emotion is designed to help you define how you feel, not control how you live or respond to how you feel. Emotions are like an alarm clock that says okay, something's happening and I'm feeling a certain way. You decide where you allow your emotions to take you. You decide whether it brings you into anxiety. You decide where you allow your emotions to take you from anger to rage, etc. It's literally your decision.

What do you do when you're prompted? Jesus when prompted with sorrow and grief went to his prayer partners to pray for him. He didn't run into a cave of seclusion or allow it to manifest into depression. He went to his prayer partners, his disciples. He went to God. Being emotional is determined or actuated by emotion rather than reason. Do you have a lifestyle where you're guided by emotion rather than reason? Reason is defined as the basis of motive for an action, decision, or conviction, a declaration made to explain or justify action, decision, or conviction. You know what's funny, we use emotion in the same way.

We use it to justify actions, decisions, and conviction. Even emotion and reason work on the same frequency. When you try to do something right, you have the conviction, in the actions and in the decision making, which shows that you model reasoning. In the same way, when your conviction is based off your emotions, your decision making, and your actions will model that too.

So, a lady's boyfriend made her mad, so she scratched cuss words in his car. So, she made him mad, and he became abusive. When you operate in reason and your boyfriend makes you mad, you would say, let's just walk away for a minute so I can get myself together. Maybe your girlfriend makes you mad, and she says babe I'm sorry because you modeled biblical principles. That said, love covers a multitude of sins. So, in love, I'm going to apologize and just say, I'm sorry. For the sake of love, they both operate on the same frequency. A lot of things we do in life operate on the same frequency.

The word emotion itself is defined as a mental state that arises spontaneously and is often accompanied by psychological changes or a feeling. It happens when we least expect it. No one sits around and says, you know what, today I want to be mad so I'm going to focus on being mad. Nope, something happens out of nowhere. This is very important because that's what happened to Jesus. They were headed into the garden and grief pops in his spirit. The same way that we have certain emotions spontaneously arise, we must have a spontaneous reaction. No! I'm not going to allow this emotion to manifest and mature in me. I'm going to pray.

Emotions involve three distinct components: a subjective experience, a physiological response, and a behavioral or expressive response. A subjective response experience refers to emotional and cognitive impact of human experience. It's basically saying that when you went through something you experienced it in a moment, whether it be major such as rape or molestation or as simple as not getting a raise. This refers to the emotional and cognitive impact that happens in your mind, will, and emotions when you have an experience. Physiological responses are the bodies automatic reactions to a stimulus such as dizziness, dry mouth, faster breathing, adrenaline rush, nausea, panic attacks, shaking, and sweating. These physiological responses are things that should alert you. I'm giving you some natural concepts, by trying to give you some biblical principle taken from the text. So, when you see this stuff starting to manifest and your body starting to respond with the sweating, this should be your sign that you need to start praying for yourself or call your prayer partner.

The next step is the expressive response, i.e., expressing the emotion or the outward expression of emotion. There are basic emotions that are universally experienced in our human culture such as happiness, sadness, fear, anger, pride, embarrassment, and excitement. So, the experience will send a signal to your body a lot of times and your body has a response that alerts you of an experience causing an expressive response and emotion. You need to take these natural signals and start praying in that moment, not just sit there. You need to break that yoke and say in the name of Jesus, I will not panic. I will not have an attack; I'm going to trust in the Lord. I'm not going to lean on my own understanding concerning this experience and this physiological response. I'm not going to allow this thing to manifest into a greater realm of emotion and expressing it through facial expressions and communication. You say you're alright, but your tone and facial expressions say you're not.

In scripture reason looks like, "You shall know the truth and the truth will make you free" (John 8:32 KJV). Notice that in that passage it says make you free. When you are operating in truth, you have no choice. It will make you free. When you are operating in truth, truth has to be your first response in emotional situations. You may have lived your whole life around a bad experience, and you are overly protective of your kids because something happened to you. They can't even play sports because you are afraid that something bad will happen to them like it did to you. That's called emotional response, opposed to operating in reason and the truth. Philippians 4:11 KJV says; "Not that I speak a respect of want for I have learned, in whatsoever state I am, therewith to be content." Please note that contentment is in God. It's in God's ability. He said for God so love the world that he gave his only begotten son, that if I believe in him, I will not perish. Which means I won't expire, wither, rot, or vanish. He's not going to let my soul spoil.

Another definition for perish is to die or be destroyed, especially in a violent or untimely manner. If I believe in God, I won't be destroyed. I won't think about being destroyed. I won't have destructive thoughts, but I'll have everlasting life. Life defined biblically a lot of times is God being active in your life. So, I won't perish. But I'll have godly activity constantly activating in my life, and it'll be everlasting. It won't stop. Some individuals read John 3:16, focusing solely on heaven, yet overlooking the profound relevance of those words here on earth. That's why Jesus said, 'When you pray, pray like this: Thy will be done on earth as it is in heaven.' If you believe in Him, your life won't spawn, deteriorate, die, or be destroyed; instead, it will have everlasting life. It will be active with God all through it. I feel His presence; I know He exists because He's all in me, around me, and flowing through me.

Now, go back to the text. Jesus said, 'The spirit is always willing.' Because of religion and tradition, some people have not been taught to think that way. You've been taught to beg God instead of knowing that God exists. You've been taught to give up and fight in your flesh instead of surrendering to God and letting Him handle it. Paul said in Philippians 4:11, 'I've learned whatever state I'm in, to be content.' The definition of content is peace of mind, mental or emotional satisfaction being mentally or emotionally satisfied with things as they are and being willing to accept circumstances, a proposed course of action, or a peace of mind.

CLOSING PRAYER

Emotionally me. Father, I thank you for tonight. I thank you, Father God, that you give us beauty for ashes and joy his blessing instead of morning, festive praise instead of despair. According to Isaiah 61 and three, Lord, I thank you, Father God, that tonight we will no longer operate from a dysfunctional, emotional understanding of life, but will now be guided through a healthy perspective of emotions and being the emotional Father God that they come to alert us, not destroy us, not guide us. But you gave it to us so that we could feel because throughout the scriptures, Father God, you showed us that you feel a certain way concerning us. You created us Lord, and you said we were good. Father God, you created us Father God, and you called us good lord. You created us in your image. And so, you said I feel, so I'm going to let you feel for God.

You so, loved the world that he gave his only begotten, Father, I thank you, Lord, that You made us just like you. But you've called us to be in control of our emotions, just like you. And so, Father, I thank you that tonight someone will be free. And that they are functioning from a realm of reason, oppose to be led by reason and truth, the truth of the matter. Thank You, Lord, the truth of the matter, and the truth of what your Word says concerning them. opposed to their emotions. Father, I thank you and we denounce every spirit of disfunction of anger, sadness, disgust, fear, pride, shame, embarrassment that comes to taunt them and every other bad emotion that they've allowed to guide them. Father, you say that you have no other God before you and so father we denounce the ill thinking that would allow emotions to heal... I have so much priority before you that we allow them to become our God. Father, I thank you that liberty is their portion. We forever give you the praise, the glory and the honor in Jesus' name, Amen.

Emotional Me Check-In: How are you Feeling?

Find a quiet space to reflect and invite God into your time of prayer. Use the **Emotional Me Check-In** questionnaire to honestly assess your feelings, their triggers, and any Scripture that speaks to them. Release your emotions to God, seek peace, and consider any actions, like reconciliation or serving others. Reach out for support if needed, and close with gratitude.

1. What am I feeling right now? Can I name this emotion before God?

2. How would I describe this feeling in prayer to God?

3. What does the Bible say about this kind of emotion?

4. How could trusting God impact the way I respond to this emotion?

5. What step can I take to seek peace, healing, or forgiveness in relation to this feeling?

NOTES

Chapter Two

THE WARFARE OF EMOTIONS

God gave us emotions, but if you look at Galatians 5:22-23, one of the main fruits of the spirit, that we need to possess is self-control. Depending on the version you read, meaning that being a spirit being in a fleshy body, we must learn a realm of self-control to control this fleshly nature. God gave us emotions, but he told us to have self-control over our emotions. His desire for us as spirit beings in a fleshly body was that we would embrace being called Christians. If you embrace being called a Christian, profess Christianity, and you abide by Christian principles, there should be a piece of you that says, I'm supposed to control my emotions, not let my emotions control me because I possess the spirit of self-control. As a believer, controlling my emotions is my mandate. Your mandate, as a believer is to take authority of your emotions. All of us have emotions, God gave us emotions, but our emotions weren't supposed to define who we were.

You know people say this is just how I feel, this is just who I am. No, you are not supposed to be your emotional self. You are not supposed to be overwhelmed and overtaken by emotions. You are supposed to feel but not be frustrated. You are supposed to feel but not be consumed. You are supposed to feel but not be moved. You are supposed to feel but not shift into sin. He said be angry, but sin not. He says it's okay to feel that emotion called anger, but make sure it doesn't go overboard and cause you to sin. Make sure you don't meditate on that thing and let it become priority in your thought patterns. Make sure it doesn't control that moment, minute, or whole day where it becomes a place of self-consumption. You've consumed so much to the point where you are nothing but a ball of anger. Make sure that doesn't have you to the point where everything you do it comes from your anger.

You're mad at everyone and no one knows why you're mad at them. You try to ruin other people's day because you're mad. Some people say misery loves company. Well sometimes emotionalism loves company too. You go around looking for everybody to feed off your emotion and be emotional with you. It becomes such a system for you that you learn to operate and manipulate people by and through your emotion. That need for affirmation and comfort drives you. You take your emotional self to more emotional people with hopes that they'll put a Band-Aid on your emotional wound. You learn to build a lifestyle of emotionalism. That's your first response to the point where it becomes your idol. That's what he's talking about. He says be angry and sin not. He's saying don't allow this to become an idol or become your god where you cross over into this realm called sin. That means this emotion got you so caught up that you separate yourself from God.

You're going to be mad at God and frustrated with him to the point where you operate from around that leads you into this thing called sin. You are cussing people out and start talking bad to people because you didn't operate from around with self-control that would keep you in alignment with salvation and righteousness. You don't carry self-control; you don't embrace a realm of self-control because you don't embrace this realm of meekness. You know love and because it's been such a bad habit for you that you've embraced for quite some time. You become okay with this posture.

I'm a man that suffered with anger, life, and experiences. I allowed that stuff to consume me for a long time until I was challenged from a realm of teaching and counsel there calls me to reevaluate myself. So, God wants you to stay in this spot so that you are challenged in your way of thinking and your dysfunction. It would cause your eyes to be open to the new thing God wants to do in your psyche called behold, be healthy. My hope is this would challenge you to fix that thing; to own that space, and to turn around, because you don't must be emotional me. You don't must be that unless you choose to be. Sometimes as believers we put that thing off on deliverance but sometimes it's just you. When the dream is gone but you still embrace the thoughts, it's just you. When the experience has passed, but you are still stuck, it's just you. You're still struggling in certain areas. You're married but you still have the trauma of all the past hurts and past relationships. Now everything you defined in your spouse is based on all the trauma you went through with your last. You still choose to hold on.

    I remember I couldn't come out of the lifestyle of the thug life. Everything I did I navigated through the lens of who I was as a drug addict, a dealer, a thief, a burglar, and everything else I used to be before salvation. My way of thinking was guided through the lens of who I was, not who I am. What I went through, not where I am now. My pain and suffering through experiences and not the life that God had given me in freedom, liberty, and the Holy Ghost. How I judged people and carried myself around people was through the lens of balled up emotions from experiences. So, I was Kirk. The confused, angry, hard to get along with, hard to get to know, hard to connect with, hard to grow with, hard to build relationship with Kirk. Everything looked like it was defined by what I've been through. The reality is I'm no longer in that place. Once I realized I wasn't there I didn't must identify with the trauma of the experience because that moment happened then and I'm living in the now. I don't must live now according to what happened back then.

When people always come with the butts, my response is but you don't want to heal. You're not giving yourself the chance to heal. You're not ready to move on from that place. You're not ready to mature. You're not ready to grow. You're not willing to grow. You're not willing to accept the liberty that God has given you now. You're looking at a dude that's been molested. You're looking at a dude that suffered from every relationship issue. You are looking at a dude that suffered from the trauma of drug abuse. When my wife got to Texas, people started telling her who I was, but her only response was, I don't see that on you though. Even just the other day we ran into a retired policeman in Home Depot, and I have this running thing but it's an inside joke for us. The inside joke is that I was his first police chase when he entered the force. And the other day, he told my wife the story and I couldn't believe he still remembered. He even remembered the alias name I gave him hoping he would move on before I took off running. I'm not mad about it because I'm over it. I'm not there. I've been free and set apart and delivered from that lifestyle, the streets, and street culture for 20 years. So, it doesn't bother me.

It's amazing how such a traumatic time in my life can be funny and can even be used to encourage others not to live in that place anymore. I hope you hear what I'm saying. I'm not only here trying to tell my business I'm trying to tell somebody that you can move on. You can move beyond traumatic situations in your life. Revelations 12:11 says, "We all will come by the blood of the lamb but also by the word of your testimony". Some of you haven't fully overcome by the lamb so you can't tell your testimony because it's still emotionally tense for you.

OPEN PRAYER

So, Father thank you for all you do. I thank you Father God for the subject of emotional me the warfare of emotion. And so, Father, I thank you that tonight you reveal strategy concerning the warfare of emotion. I thank you that you expose the enemy and his devices. I thank you that someone will be set free. I thank you that someone will be delivered. I thank you that someone will have a new outlook on life. Thank you, Lord, I just feel a refreshing that will come from a reading this chapter. I even sense that someone is already being refreshed. Father, I thank you so much. I thank you father. And forever give you the praise, the glory, in the honor in Jesus name, Amen.

In this chapter, we're going to discuss the warfare of emotion, exploring the principles outlined in 2 Corinthians 10:4-5. The passage states, "For the weapons of our warfare are not carnal, but mighty through God, to the pulling down of strongholds, casting down imaginations, and every high thing that exalteth itself against the knowledge of God, and bringing into captivity every thought to the obedience of Christ."

Paul visited the Corinthian church with a mandate to call them back into right standing with God. Despite their spiritual gifts, they lacked character and engaged in carnal behaviors. Paul confronted them, aiming to guide them back into a proper relationship with God. During this period, the Corinthian church challenged Paul's apostleship. Due to his bold, courageous, strong, and stern approach, some accused Paul of walking in the flesh, deeming him as carnal. However, when Paul referenced God, he intended for them to understand the severity of the nature in which they were operating.

> It's your decision whether you give your emotion access which is attached to the carnal response to some warfare

In the scripture, they're challenging him, and in return, Paul is letting them know that while he does walk in the flesh and has a carnal nature, he doesn't fully embrace his flesh because he understands there is a spiritual nature in him that takes priority. Paul was essentially saying, "I acknowledge I have a flesh, but I don't engage with it because I understand that the weapons of my warfare are not carnal. I cannot fight a carnal war in a carnal way. I can't use the same tools and artillery that the world employs when it rises against me. I can't employ the same methods because I am God's man. When life presents challenges, I can't approach them with a fleshly state of mind because I am devoted to God."

They were attacking him, and instead of the breastplate of righteousness, they fought with the image of success. Instead of the shoes of the gospel of peace, they fought with smooth words. Instead of the shield of faith, they fought with their perception of power. Instead of the helmet of salvation, they fought with lording over authority. Instead of the sword of the spirit, they fought with human schemes and programs.

Paul was challenging them to change because he saw that they tended to rely on and admire carnal weapons for a spiritual battle. Paul understood Ephesians 6:16-19 where he said, "Hold up the shield of faith to stop the fiery arrows of the devil. Put on the salvation as your helmet and take the sword of the spirit, which is the word of God. Always pray in the spirit and on every occasion. Stay alert and be present in your prayers for all believers everywhere."

Paul understood that Ephesians 6:16-18 was an equation for spiritual warfare; he also knew that they cared nothing of it. Instead of the helmet of salvation, they wanted to lord over people's lives, and they wanted to be the lord over salvation. They sought to determine the deciding factor based on how they presented their ideas, schemes, and manipulation.

One of the things I want you to pay attention to is that we have the Corinthian church trying to get a fleshly rise out of Paul. For emotions to arise in you, there must be a war lost in your life. For emotions to manifest in a moment, there must first be a war. Warfare is defined as an active struggle between competing entities, a price of war, or a war of wits, diplomatic warfare.

So, you have a spirit being trying to take control and a fleshly being also trying to take control within one body. Basically, this is a spirit being in a carnal being, always vying for control over one body. Then there is a spiritual nature, a divine nature, and the God nature in you, seeking to have full control and operate fully in the same body. It's your decision whether you give your emotions access, which is attached to the carnal response to some warfare happening in your life, or to the spirit nature. Both need permission.

I mentioned in the last chapter that fear and faith operate off the same paradigm. They both need you to believe. That's the equivalent; fear and faith, the spiritual and the carnal. They both need you to believe in them for them to have full access in your life and to your life.

Earlier, I mentioned that before emotions arise, there must be a struggle between competing entities. Most times, when the emotional response happens, it's because you've given permission to your carnal nature, which is attached to experiences, trauma, issues, struggles, hurt, and pain. You've given them permission, and when you do that, you stir up all that emotion. Why? Because when your emotion has fully overtaken you, it takes over your ability to reason. Now you're overthinking it, and your emotion can turn into sin; sadness can turn to depression, anger can turn to rage.

What we don't realize is that things continue until death is finished. Lust is not just something sexual; lust is you coming into covenant with a thought, and then it becomes sin, which is the action, bringing forth death, which is the consequent separation from God.

A lot of times, sadness turns to depression. Sadness is the lust, and depression is the sin. The action is death. So, what's the action of depression that most people run to? Thoughts of suicide. So, you were sad, then you got depressed. Now, you're ready to commit suicide. You came into agreement with the thought that was sent on assignment to attack you, and you were in warfare. Unfortunately, you didn't win the struggle. Sin was conceived in the thought.

When you can't control your thoughts, which is the lust, it becomes sin. Sin is the emotional response of acting on how you feel in your emotion, which brings forth death. So, anger brought forth rage because he was mad at his spouse, and then he saw a gun nearby, which brought forth literal death. So, there were two deaths: that person and your relationship with God. It's an active struggle between competing entities. Your spirit and your sin nature want control of you.

If you believe that I don't have emotional moments, I do. I have just learned how to wage a good war. I'm always attacked by something. If you have a sin nature, you have warfare. You just won't see me emotionally respond because the Holy Spirit has graced me with a capacity to embrace self-control. I say to myself, "This isn't God; I'm not acting out on this. He doesn't want me depressed or sad." So, why do we continue an insane cycle of embracing things that we know God doesn't want for us?

I would say I am a loser, an outcast. I spent a decade in drug addiction and still counted myself as that old thug. Ten years free, but I wasn't free in my mind because I didn't fully embrace the principles that wanted control over my life. See, when you start embracing the spirit nature, you embrace things like 2 Corinthians 5:17 that says, "In Christ, I'm a new creature; old things have passed away, behold, all things have become new."

When you fully embrace it, you understand that He died on the cross, so you don't have to relive it. When you fully embrace the thought patterns that you've been washed white as snow, you can look at Psalm 23 and say, "Lord, thank you for restoring my soul. I thank you for leading me beside the still waters. I thank you that you're my shepherd who guides me. My emotions don't have to guide me because the Lord is my shepherd. I shall not want for anything. I don't have to want for sanity. He gave me sanity because He decided to lead me beside the still waters and restore my soul."

See, David was saying he doesn't have to flow in and out of his emotions when he knows God is in his life. He was writing a song to God, letting Him know, "Lord, I love it when you're near and you guide me. You don't have to be double-minded. You don't have to overthink anything. You don't have to be confused about that thing because God said His word won't return to you void, and you're His child, so it won't return to you void either. It will accomplish the healing and wholeness you desire. It will accomplish that freedom you desire. It will accomplish that liberty. It was accomplished on the cross, and He's still accomplishing it now."

I don't have to love my wife based on trauma from past relationships. I don't have to look over my wife's shoulder. I don't have to see if she operates like others did in past relationships because I prayed for her. I prayed 1 John 4:18, "There is no fear in love, when it's perfect love, godly love." I'm operating in love from a godly principal-type love, Corinthians 13-type love. That love will cast out all fear in my relationship because fear has torment. Plus, in 1 John 4:18, the Bible says that fear is not made perfect in love. So, how can you expect to have mature love when you operate in fear, i.e., your flesh?

Couples just torment each other because they stay in the flesh, lacking communication skills. They lack honor, respect, and don't know how to walk away when they need to. They don't know how to be quiet when they need to. They both have false expectations of each other and can carry this into any relationship, including with a supervisor, friend, or family.

There's a warfare going on in people with Sadie competing for your life. I mentioned John 316 said, "God so loved the world that he gave his only begotten son that whosoever would believe in him would

> The warfare of emotion and how you perceive the warfare will determine whether you're in a struggle or a fight.

not perish." You've been called to believe so you won't perish. If you just believe, your soul wouldn't perish. If you just embrace the concept of believing even though we don't feel right, things seem funny, and stuff is happening in your life, you won't perish.

You don't have to perish; He said you'd have everlasting life. Satan is competing for that one thing—everlasting life. He hopes you think on all things that are carnal, fleshly, and sinful, as opposed to divine and righteous. He hopes that you'll dwell on the drama instead of the truth because he wants you to pay more attention to the trauma. Then he can cloud your judgment concerning the truth. So, when you can't navigate to the truth, you must question your judgment. You must question your ability to think positively when the truth is not your response to the warfare. That's why I said you need to know the truth. Why? Because it will make you free. He didn't say hopefully you'll be free. He said it will make you free. "Trust in the Lord with all your heart, lean not on your understanding; in all your ways submit to him, and he will make your paths straight" (Proverbs 3:5-6, NIV).

I said at the beginning, warfare operates in two paradigms. There are two definitions. One is the acts taken to destroy the struggle and acts taken to destroy or undermine the strength of another (freedictionary.com).

I get tired of people talking about warfare. It's not so much the warfare as it is the perception of the warfare. The warfare of emotion and how you perceive the warfare will determine whether you're in a struggle or a fight. The dictionary basically tells us you can either focus on the struggle or you can focus on how you're going to destroy it. In other words, you can focus on your fleshly attachment to the struggle. The higher the level, the bigger the devil, and the more you focus on the struggle in your mind. You focus on the struggle of warfare instead of the act of warfare.

> **If you embrace your war, you have a lion nature in you.**

When I talk about warfare, I'm talking about deliverance. I'm talking about casting out demons. I'm talking about strategy, posture, and movement because that is in me. "Greater is he that is in me, then he that is in the world" (1 John 4:4). So now, do I really believe? What did God say? You really need to pay attention to this in scripture. When they went to Lazarus, they said the Lord was too late. He was dead. They were struggling with the realities of what was happening in the natural, but Jesus said no, he's asleep. He understood that the weapons of warfare have nothing to do with the natural but the supernatural. He understood that there's power in his tongue, and he understood that he's backed by Him. That's why he told them, and the scriptures say he could have called on legions, those angels. He understood who he is. He is the epitome of acting, undertaking, destroying, and undermining the strength of the enemy. He understood that the devil is like a lion, and he is the lion. I need you to understand that because you have the spirit of God in you, you are a lion. He's acting like a lion. If you embrace your war, you have a lion nature in you.

So, Jesus said, "Roll the stone away." God wants you to know that you can roll the stone away. He says, "Roll the stone away because I am life. I'm like abundantly, and I don't care if he looked dead, but life abundantly just walked on the scene. Jesus just walked on the scene and said because in me you can have being, I'm going to call you forward, Lazarus, so you can be. God is saying roll away the stone and let the stink out. There is freshness and newness of who he's calling you to be. You don't have to keep the tomb closed and locked up inside of you.

So, there are two functions of warfare. One relates to the struggle of warfare, and the other relates to you defeating the struggle by acting. Let me give you two definitions for carnal. Thefreedictionary.com defines carnal as, pertaining to or characterized by the passions and appetites of the flesh or body. The second definition is spiritual, temporal, worldly.

You have a struggle between your passions and appetites of your fleshly nature and temporal things. That's why loneliness is a prominent thing that strikes up in believers because God wants to be their father. He wants to be your bridegroom. He wants to be your husband, but those temporal moments and that desire for that being a lot of times get the best of us. So, there's a war between being lonely and being single in that moment. There's a struggle between you desiring to be chased and doing the chasing. Carnal, according to the Greek term, is having the nature of flesh, i.e., under the control of animal appetites. So, he's connecting your passions and appetites to animal nature. Number two says, having it seen in the animal nature or aroused by the animal nature.

Many of us have seen pit bulls and how out of control they can be at times. Now, I love pit bulls. I used to raise and breed them for a long time. So, I know they can be controlled. I'm talking about pit bulls that haven't been properly trained or wild animals. If you haven't been trained, you're just a wild animal, and carnality is likened to an animal nature, untamed, and uncontrolled. If you watch Animal Planet or National Geographic, animals like lions and bears are guided by the need to hunt and feed. Your carnal nature is guided by a need to hunt and feed on your desires. That's why Jesus said, just believe, all things are possible, because he understands your carnal nature. Why? Because he was born into a carnal nature. God put himself into flesh, and he understands. Look at how Judah was unable to contain that desire for money anymore.

The only thing that can contain your carnal nature is your spirit of nature. So, examine yourself before you start reaching out to people for reinforcement. That's one of the major areas of warfare; to act on that thing, not deal with the struggle. Take the strength away from it so it doesn't have you. If you connect with people who haven't been prayed up, you will just transfer the struggle to them. When everyone is in emotional state, crying, weeping, and wallowing, it is not beneficial or helpful to anyone. So, when the struggle pops up, you should go into a different realm of warfare and try to figure out how to take the strength away from it, acts undertaken to destroy it. What do I need to do to destroy this thing?

It all goes back to embracing God or embracing your flesh. Will you embrace God or the situation? Your God nature and your fleshly nature are competing in that moment. That's the warfare. You want to behold the things of God, but this thing seems to keep getting the best of you. So now you must rise above the moment and embrace your authority. You must learn to rise above it because your emotions are governed by that animal nature without self-control. The experienced trauma, hurt, molestation, and rape are all governed by your carnal nature, which is likely the uncontrolled appetites. That's why when you get mad, you want to talk out of character. A person's action doesn't require a reaction; you lack self-control. You're not aligning with spirituality and Kingdom thinking.

Here, Paul is saying the weapons of our warfare are not carnal, but they are great in power, skillful, strong, and forceful through God. He said you can't be in control of the war without self-control. In essence, if you use God, he will give you the power. He'll give you the skill and strength to have such a divine force to tear down the stronghold. What is the stronghold? It is the area dominated or occupied by something, or it is the area that you've been given permission to have more priority in that moment. God has the power to tear down that stuff. Blue Letter Bible defines it as the things in which mere human confidence is imposed. Isn't it funny how when something is weighing on you, it feels like you can't win the battle? You feel like you don't have the confidence to survive it or the power to move past it. You feel like it's so overwhelming that you can't overcome it because a stronghold is designed to impose on your confidence. You've let that thing in so much that it built a fortress, which is another term for stronghold. It built a fortress around your emotion and locked you in right there. The warfare of emotion and how you perceive the warfare will determine whether you're in a struggle or a fight.

Strongholds are anything on which one relies. Sometimes we get to the point where we rely on our strongholds. We rely on the struggles we have in our flesh. We're so accustomed to struggling and not fighting that we ruin beautiful things in our lives like marriages, relationships with kids, employers, coworkers, family and friends. But he says our weapons are mighty; they have great power, skill, and strength to forcefully come against the attack of the enemy. Paul is telling them, "You know what? I hear you're trying to attack who I am as an apostle, but number one, it's not going to rouse my emotions. Number two, you're not going to get me to cross over into the realm of lack of confidence. What you're going to do is stir up my ability to destroy this carnal realm that you operate in and this carnal attack you try to impose on my life." He said, "But they're mighty through God to the pulling down of strongholds, casting down imaginations" (2 Corinthians 5:10, NLT). Casting out demons means to throw forcefully, not gently. So, when you feel sad, don't say, "I'm going to put the sadness over here." No, take it and throw it out.

> Now that the wound is healed, you must give yourself the grace to be healed in your mind.

When you are operating from a spiritual paradigm, God will forcefully move not like him out of the way, casting down imaginations. Imagination is defined as the ability to form mental images of things that are not present to the senses and are not considered real (freedictionary.com). So, in essence it's your ability to operate in a false sense of reality. You've allowed your emotions to create a false narrative, or a false sense of reality and you live in that space. Yet, because real life is in Christ, it will cast down any false sense of reality forcefully if we embrace Christ and not the struggle. Choose the acts of destroying the attack, instead of embracing the struggle in the attack. some of us allow our emotions to go to a realm of dysfunction, where we create a false reality and instead of operating from a realm of truth, we live in this false reality that nothing's ever going to change.

We limit God's power to change things that you alone will never change. Saying and believing things like, "I will never change," "This is who I am," or "I'm just me," you're saying you really don't want to change, and you're living in this false sense of reality that you're healthy and whole. It's you who needs counseling. It's you who needs to change. When you are in your emotions, you leave reason for a false reality. When you stay stuck there, you say to God, that delivering me, saving me, and setting me free is no longer my reality, but my emotion. But God said, have no other idols before me. In essence, your emotions become an idol that takes more priority over God's ability to change your situation.

Imagination is the ability to form mental images of things that are not present. You keep seeing and flashing the rape, the trauma, the abuse in your head when the person is no longer there to hurt you. The abuser is no longer there, and it doesn't have to live in your present moment in time; it doesn't have to be real to you anymore. But you look in the mirror and see the scars and the trauma, not realizing they represent a healed wound. Now that the wound is healed, you must give yourself the grace to be healed in your mind. God wants to heal your mind. Romans 12:2 says, "Be not conformed to this world, but be transformed by the renewing of your mind." You don't have to stay in the same place in your mind. You don't have to be conformed to this world; you don't have to be conformed to the experience or the trauma. You don't have to be conformed to the situation or the divorce. You don't have to be conformed to the verbal or physical abuse. You don't have to be conformed to the molestation. You don't have to be conformed to the fact that you didn't have a mom or dad, but you can be transformed by the renewing of your mind.

Oftentimes we build this false sense of reality instead of paying attention to reality. You should say to yourself, yes it happened but I'm healed, and God didn't let me die. God didn't let me leave this earth early, but he left me here with a purpose. Now if I could only see the test as a testimony and my story as something that has the capacity to set somebody else free. if I can only see the moments and situations as a training ground instead of trauma. God is teaching me how to go through this so I can help somebody. People went to college to understand how to counsel people who suffered drug abuse and others just used drugs and overcame. Sadly, experience is the best degree you can have. Think of a scale with 0 in the middle, 123 on the right, - 1 - 2 - 3 on the left. You started at 0 but your trauma resulted in a negative impact and placed you at - 3. The steps you took to overcome created positives in your life and changed your narrative. This created new thought patterns of being free in Christ.

Negative impact			Neutral			Change the narrative
←						→
-1	-2	-3	0	1	2	3

Just like Paul in this text, in life people will use things and situations to try to evaluate you and show you that you aren't who God says you are, hoping to get a carnal or emotional response. Yet, when you understand that the weapons of your warfare are in God and are mighty, you come out of that false reality into reality. That God has to become your reality. Have you ever heard of false evidence appearing real? That's what fear really is. It's kind of like the kid who you try to hand some chicken, but they're used to a bottle, so they don't want it. I tried to hand my daughter some chicken once, and she cried like somebody burned her up with fire. I made her eat the chicken because in her head it was going to be gross. After all of that, she started chewing the chicken. Suddenly, all I heard was yummy daddy, this is yummy. Right now, I'm trying to serve this meal that may not seem like it tastes right, but if you learn to act out the principles in this book, learn how to apply his word, then you'll be able to say, "Oh taste and see that the Lord is good" (Psalm 34:8). See, that's what my daughter said when she ate that chicken, yummy, yummy, yummy. Oh, taste and see that the Lord is good, and forgiveness is the key that removes vain imaginations. When you can forgive people for what happened to you and forgive yourself, the false reality has no space because freedom comes when you're able to forgive, and challenge moments with truth.

CLOSING PRAYER

Heavenly Father, I thank you for what you've done. I thank you that there will be those who are able to cast down imaginations from this day forward. Father, I thank you that they are no longer emotionally bound, but that their perception is changed tonight, concerning warfare. I pray that they will no longer talk about the struggle, but they'll talk about the opportunity to destroy the struggle, gain divine strength from the Kingdom of God, and annihilate the struggle between the divine nature and their carnal nature.

Father, just like Paul said in the text, I have carnal moments, but they don't define me. I read from a Kingdom paradigm. Father, I thank you that they realize that even though they are in this world, they don't have to be of it. Father, I thank you that the warfare of emotions will turn into warring warriors that destroy emotional attacks. Father, I thank you that we kill those animal-type appetites that come to navigate and guide them through realms of lacking control over their thought patterns.

Father, we bind that thing up in this hour and we place it at the feet of Christ to be cleansed by the blood of the lamb. Father, that the paradigm of operating from vain imaginations and a false sense of reality will now be cleansed and made whole. That they come into a reality that you are their reality. Father, I thank you that they'll come into agreement with your principles concerning them. I thank you that they'll come into agreement with your mandate concerning them. I thank you that they'll embrace Galatians 5:22-23 concerning them, that the fruits of the spirit would manifest in them more and more.

I thank you that love will continue and that it would be a fixed practice that they will never let love fail because love covers a multitude of sins. Father God, I thank you that as love covers the sins of the abusers and attackers, that they'll find it in themselves to forgive them and let you have your way in their lives. I thank you that they become more pliable to your will and not the carnal will. I pray they'll be more pliable to your principle and your word when the struggle of warfare rises up within them.

I thank you that they'll grab hold of that Kingdom authority and that they'll be in Christ. Father, I pray that even as according to Ephesians 6:16-18, that they will put on the shield of faith, salvation as their helmet, and take the sword of the spirit which is the word of God. It is my prayer that we always pray in the spirit, on every occasion, stay alert and be persistent in prayer for all believers everywhere. I pray they will be your man and your woman, Kingdom-minded. In Jesus' name, I pray, Amen and thank God.

Emotional Me Check-In: How are you Feeling?

Find a quiet space to reflect and invite God into your time of prayer. Use the **Emotional Me Check-In** questionnaire to honestly assess your feelings, their triggers, and any Scripture that speaks to them. Release your emotions to God, seek peace, and consider any actions, like reconciliation or serving others. Reach out for support if needed, and close with gratitude.

1. What am I feeling right now? Can I name this emotion before God?

2. How would I describe this feeling in prayer to God?

3. What does the Bible say about this kind of emotion?

4. How could trusting God impact the way I respond to this emotion?

5. What step can I take to seek peace, healing, or forgiveness in relation to this feeling?

NOTES

Chapter Three

WOUNDS AND SCARS

OPENING PRAYER

Heavenly father, I thank you for what you'll do in the lives of the believers. Father, I thank you that even as we talk about the topic emotional me, wounds, and scars, that somebody would be guided to a realm of healing and deliverance and be set free. Father, I thank you that you know the thoughts concerning each person that reads this book. You know the areas of struggle, the areas that they need healing and deliverance. Father, I thank you that the words that flow from heaven are released exactly how you desire them to father, you are the great physician. Father, we decree and declare that surgery will be performed in many areas of their lives, that they've been praying for and asking for a great release. Father, we thank you and we love you. We ask that you do what love does, heal. Thank you, Lord in Jesus name, Amen.

Someone shared this revelation, and it really stuck with me. We were on Facebook live and they were talking about toxic reproduction as it pertains to people being hurt in ministry. Leaders have been constantly reproducing and trying to build ministries and reproducing disciples from a toxic paradigm. In the middle of that conversation, we were talking about wounds and scars when they dropped a bomb on us. It was said that wounds represent you not being healed, and scars represent you being healed. That just sat with me for about three weeks. That really ministered to me as I have been focusing on the topic of emotional me.

So, the first chapter of emotional me was the foundation how God gave us emotions, but they weren't supposed to have control over us. He desires that we have control over them as it pertains to Galatians 5:22-23, self-control being one of the fruits of the spirit. His desire is that we would process our emotions in a healthy way. In chapter 2 I talked about the warfare of emotion and how they at times take us on a roller coaster ride. We try to learn how to fight off those thoughts and bring them into subjection, using self-control and the principles given to us in the scripture. The thought came to mind that a lot of times we leave the fight or warfare with wounds and scars. In this chapter we're going to talk about emotional me from the notion of wounds and scars. Sometimes even though you go through the warfare and win the battle, you lose the war. We must learn to win both the battle and war.

Most times it's going to be what you do with your wounds and scars. We started to raise up people that want one of two things, either they want to find a way to avoid the wound, or they want clearance to be out of control emotionally because of the wound. The Bible says that he was wounded for our transgressions, and we are called to be Christ like in the earth. Wounds are a part of the journey as well. People want deliverance to be something that's happy and joyful, and it gets to that on some days. Most of the time deliverance is shining a light on the places that you're bound in. That's not comfortable, it's not nice and not is it enjoyable.

Sometimes we are emotionally out of control and want people to give us permission to be, or we put on this facade that we're in control, but the reality of a wound is that it shows up when you least expect it. You don't go into a fight expecting to get wounded. You hope you don't get wounded but at some point, when they connect with you, that eye turns black, and you see a wound there. Now you must explain. See what happens is when people notice in the spiritual realm and discern your spiritual black eye, you want permission to be out of control. The reality of the wound is that we start trying to embrace the mindset of, "This is just who I am," or "It doesn't define me." The thing is when we get around people, we want them to embrace the wound when we are called to move towards healing. So, you hide in the body of Christ, and then get around a leader who has discernment.

When a person gets around me talking about, "I'm an addict," I struggle with that. When we come into Christ, we realize in him we are new creatures. We don't live in the realm of once an addict always an addict because we've been set free from addiction or any influences of the enemy when we resist him. (see John 8:36). In my struggles with addiction, I realized I detoxed using the Holy Spirit. I went to rehab three times, and I still came out on drugs. So finally, I detoxed with my parents praying and laying hands on me, anointing me with oil. A few years later I still struggled with cigarette addition. The Holy spirit told me to speak in tongues for the next three weeks and he would set me free, and He did. So, when you come into that notion of wanting people's permission to act out in your emotions when they know you've been set free, you're going to have a problem. In some cases, people find themselves more addicted to the wound than they are to the drugs because if he healed the wound, the drugs would take care of itself. See when I got delivered the Holy Spirit told me, "Don't you call yourself an addict anymore because that's not who you are."

> **You can't have deliverance and familiarity.**

When we focus on the wound opposed to deliverance we'll never heal. It will serve as a reminder of the bad experience that caused it. But the Lord says, I'd rather you grab all the uncertainty of the scar than stay in the familiarity of the wound. That's what deliverance is, the uncertainty. I don't know what this scar will mean for me, but I'm going to walk through the valley of the shadow of death with faith. I must get to the place where I fear no evil. I must learn that the Lord is my shepherd. Whatever this scar represents for me, I would rather embrace it than remain in the comfortable familiarity of the wound. The wound is the familiar place. It has dictated your life far too long. How is it going to heal? You can't have deliverance and familiarity. You must pick one. Either you're going to be the victim or the warrior.

One of the consequences of holding onto a wound is that if you choose to live with it, you must continue living as a victim. Many times, sheep come to their shepherd—whether a pastor or counselor—not fully understanding the depth of pastoring and shepherding. The Bible teaches that the shepherd is responsible for your care, growth, and nurturing, acting as a watchman over your soul. While people come to us with eternity in mind, they often forget that our role is to help them in the present. We must address your current issues to ensure that when you stand before God, He doesn't say, 'Depart from me.

I can't navigate through life and make decisions based on the time I was five. I already tried that. I was molested by a guy, but I didn't end up in the realm that the devil leaves most men, dealing in homosexuality. For a long time, I perceived everything through my 5-year-old self. Once I was free, I realized that the trauma of the wound had manifested itself in my perception of life. If you stay in the wound a second too long, over time, you become selfish because wounds breed selfishness. When Christ was wounded and beaten on the cross, the Pharisees came and said to him, "Save yourself" (Matthew 27:41 NIV). The enemy was hoping that the wounds would cause Jesus to abort the mission. When you're wounded and hurt, you should be selfish and take care of you right?

> **wounds will take us off course and cause us to abort the mission.**

Christ understood that he was moving out of the wound and into the scar. See we don't discern that in the process because we discern the pain and that's a part of circling the mountain of the wound. All you know is you were hurt but the reality is if it didn't kill you, it made you stronger. Wounds will keep you in what's happening to you. Wounds blind you from what God is doing for you. We blame God because we can't trace him in those moments. We understand that what held Christ to the cross was his reverence for God and the mission. The completion of the mission held him on the cross until he was finished. In my mind he was saying, "The wound won't make me give up. That's why it's important to recognize it for what it truly is.

Wound is defined as an injury to an Organism, especially in which the skin or another external surface is torn, pierced, cut, or otherwise broken. It's also an injury to the feelings or reputation (freedictionary.com). What stuck out to me was that it's always happening externally. If you look at the first definition, it's something done to an external surface. The second definition It's something that's always done externally but impacts us internally. The reality of it is wounds will take us off course and cause us to abort the mission. When you think about the notion of a wound being external, that means it happened in a moment that is probably no longer existing in your life. You moved on but the residue that stuck in your mind dictated your movement from here on out. Sometimes you don't realize that season has passed but somewhere in your mind you're stuck dealing with the feeling and how it messes with your reputation. God wants me to highlight some stuff for you so you can stop looking at the wound and look at the roots.

The wound is a sign that there is a root problem. There's an internal root problem that you are still allowing to linger in your thoughts. you don't realize wounds expose themselves in various ways. You may feel the need to be pampered, babied, or maybe you struggle with aggression, and you snap. You could have a sharp tongue when all we said was, "How are you doing today?" Maybe you deal with anxiety, and we all noticed it, but you don't because the wounds become your norm. For example, we see a three-year-old child not embracing self-control, throwing temper tantrums, and looking for a bottle. Like the child, you're looking to be coddled when you should be posturing yourself to stand firm in warfare. We'll live in denial when someone with experience or a discernment sees the wound that you don't see.

Say for example you're going to see a counselor, and the first thing they say is you're repeating the same thing over and over expecting new results, that's called insanity. The counselor then has you look at your insane way of thinking and just like the scripture says, they help you navigate into truths about each thing. The Bible says you shall know the truth and the truth will make you free. If you embrace truth, it will make you free. That's a strong word and you can bet your dollar on it, it's going to happen. Unfortunately, when we start pointing out those truths, people become uncomfortable with it. Freedom requires boldness, you must come out of denial and literally embrace the truth about who you are, what's operating in your life, and deal with it.

Wounds and scars look like: a person abused you and now you can't have good relationships because in your mind, everyone is just like them. You're always looking for the new man to act like the old one. She cheated on you, so now you struggle to embrace the realm of trust needed for healthy relationships. Now you require location sharing to trust a mate. You think this is healthy when everyone around you knows different. Now all the advice you give is inspired by your wounds. You tell the girl she needs to cheat on him. Stop and realize you're talking from your wound. You are sarcastic and condescending when someone says something you don't like not realizing you're exposing your trauma. My prayer is that people start looking in the mirror and take ownership. It doesn't matter how much the pastor prays over the fact that your boyfriend is abusive. If you leave church and go home to that crazy guy, you just accepted it right back into your life. We can't put the weight on the leaders. Leaders are assigned by God to point you back to God. You must take ownership and walk it out.

We understand that light has come into the world, but this isn't just any light—it's the kind that loves you beyond words. The truth is, our Lord and Savior loves you deeply, yet there's a glitch in the matrix. What He said condemns mankind: people love darkness. The reality is people love their wounds. You cry about it, but deep down, you hold onto it. You love it so much that you don't want to let it go. See, internal wounds plant seeds that trigger external behaviors, but we often focus on fixing the behavior instead of addressing the wound itself. If you want true deliverance from that wounded place, you have to let the Lord into your secret places. We say we want freedom from the wound, but the Bible tells us we aren't free because we secretly love it. The hardest truth is admitting that you love what's keeping you bound.

The Lord is saying that you must break free from clinging to the wound, because if you love the wound, you'll also be attached to the one who caused it. You hold onto the pain because you're in love with the demon that keeps bringing the chaos that comes with the wound. By doing this, you're subconsciously choosing bondage. You're shouting, praying for deliverance, but still choosing to remain in bondage by staying in wounded places. The Lord says you love it.

People cling to their wounds because it gives them an excuse to do what they want it justifies their actions. The truth is, you're in bondage because you love the wound, and that's what you must turn away from. If you love the wound, you'll love the one who caused it, and that path will ruin you.

People come to God with worldly perception of how to heal. The world tells us to medicate and look for something calm Like alcohol, sex, or drugs. The world tells us that we should fix ourselves by medicating the wound but not getting to the root of the wound. We need to stop looking for godly solutions from a worldly perspective. Manipulative leaders have taken that realm of itching ears, from vulnerable people who desire help and have manipulated the body of Christ. For example, when you want a healed heart, those leaders say you just need encouragement. So now you come to church hoping one of the leaders prophesied over you. Now God becomes this realm of Christianity where you're looking for a prophetic insight for encouragement instead of total healing. The pastor may speak a word of life into you, but the reality is the God who actually gives life, is still waiting for you to accept him so he can give it to you abundantly. You don't just need a piece of him you need all of him.

> How you look at the scar in this season will determine how he unveils and releases new things into your life.

When the Lord asks, 'What builder starts building a house without first counting the cost?' (Luke 14:28), He's reminding us that there's always a price. Yet, many people want the building without paying the cost. If you want healing, if you want deliverance, it's going to cost you your wound. You can't hold on to the wound and expect to be healed. We must shift our mindset. A scar is the evidence of a healed wound—it shows you went through something, but you're no longer in pain. When Thomas said, 'If this is truly the Savior, I need to see His scars' (John 20:25), it reflected that scars are a testimony of survival and healing. In the same way, some people won't believe you've been saved or set free without the testimony of your wounds turning into scars. As Revelation 12:11 says, 'They overcame by the blood of the Lamb and the word of their testimony.' Your scars are part of that testimony. A lamb must be wounded for blood to flow. You were tested by the blood of the lamb and moved to a realm of healing where you passed from test to testimony.

Some people don't even realize that when they ask to be Christ-like and accept Jesus as their Lord and Savior, they are starting a process of metamorphosis—being made new. As Paul said, 'This means that anyone who belongs to Christ has become a new person. The old life is gone; a new life has begun!' (2 Corinthians 5:17 NLT). This means that the experiences of the world have been left behind because Jesus died for them. You may have a scar, but you are no longer wounded. You don't need to check His hands; He already did that for you. You no longer have to identify as an addict; instead, see yourself as a believer. Don't think of yourself as a victim consider yourself a victor. All those past experiences have been washed away, and now you are made new. You may still see the scar, but your perspective on it has changed. How you view that scar in this season will determine how God unveils and releases new things into your life.

You can't stay in a wounded mindset while expecting God to release new things like your destiny and purpose into your life. You can't love your woundedness and love God at the same time. You can't enter a new situation while remaining attached to the old. You can't want the blood of Jesus to cleanse you while refusing to let it wash away the trauma. Do you believe that you have been made new? Are you a victim or victorious? Yes, I see the scar, but that scar represents your healing. Scars are defined as marks left on the skin after a wound has healed (TheFreeDictionary.com). They serve as a lasting reminder of past injuries, but the Bible reminds us to be aware of the enemy and his schemes. He comes to inflict pain, hoping you will internalize the wound through your emotions and feelings. This can damage your reputation, leading to self-condemnation or the condemnation of others, who may not understand your experience.

Self-condemnation affects your mind because of past experiences, leading you to believe you're worthless. You may doubt God's love for you, questioning whether He really saved and set you free. This creates toxic mindsets that you reproduce day after day if you never confront those thought patterns. What am I saying? I want to release a word that helps form a scar. When looking at the anatomy of a wound, we see that when your body feels an injury, it begins to release blood to clot it before forming a scab. Once the scab falls off, it leaves a scar. I'm trying to release the healing blood of Christ so it can penetrate the wound and help produce a scab.

Thomas needed to see where they had pierced Jesus; he said, 'I need to put my finger in the wound.' The Bible shows us that Christ presented Himself to Thomas and then held him accountable to this thing called faith, telling him that he needed to believe. So, what is the Lord doing? He is using His words to move us to a place of faith, but that's not the whole picture. The scar must come first; it has to ignite before it can cultivate your faith. Your faith is cultivated when the scar surfaces. He is saying to trade in the wound; don't hold onto it. If you do, that is just another voice telling you that God hasn't healed or delivered you. You can exchange the wound for a scar.

A person's perception is everything. How we understand and interpret a situation shapes our reality. That's why it's essential to seek wisdom, knowledge, and understanding, as these are foundational. I remember a conversation with my dad years ago when he asked me how I defined wisdom. I said it was the application of knowledge, and he replied, 'Yes, but when you're talking about God, wisdom is more than just applying knowledge; it's about applying it correctly.' That was an eye-opener for me. We can apply knowledge incorrectly and end up with the wrong outcome. With wisdom, we no longer perceive life as a cup that's half empty; instead, we see it as half full. When you start considering God's principles, you begin to declare by faith that all things work together for your good. So, do you truly perceive the wounds and scars as reminders of how God has worked in your life?

I've realized how many people I've been able to help through an experience that the Holy Spirit navigated me through during trauma. I began to view my experiences as God guiding me, educating me, and equipping me in areas that most people go to school for. I must start perceiving that God allowed me to go through these challenges to help others, not to hide them from people. When we talk about Thomas, yes, he needed to operate in more faith, but the people we minister to daily need to see our wounds and scars. They need to witness the healing of those wounds and scars to understand the testimony of the blood that cleansed us. There is a deep hunger for that among people. When we truly learn and grow in God, He will use our trauma to build us spiritually. Often, we think we're further along in our journey with God than we actually are. The Bible reminds us that we are to be transformed by the daily renewing of our mind.

My mother would remind me occasionally, that when I was ten, I came to her and said I had a dream that I ended up going out into the world and getting into a lot of trouble, but God came and brought me back. I saved all the people that were out there with me. I'm seeing this happen in my life. I couldn't fathom why this happened to me until I started reading scriptures. Paul was in prison saying, "I want to be with you so I may impart some spiritual gift to you" (Romans 1:11 NIV). Paul was still learning how to do the work of the ministry even though he was in a traumatic state. I'm trying to paint a picture of perception on how we need to think as believers. Jesus was on the cross nailed looking at the man to his left saying, this day you're dine with me in paradise, right?

In the book of Jeremiah 30:17, he says, "For I will restore health unto thee, and I will heal thee of thy wounds, saith the Lord." God has made you a promise, in other words, he's going to heal you and restore you of all your wounds. What I'm saying is perception is everything in the word, God's word is true, let every man be a lie. When you read his promises are you really receiving in your heart that he'll take your money and restore it and heal you. Sometimes people feel like we harp too long on the wound, and they just want us to teach on healing. The reality of the wound and the scar is if we don't identify the trauma, you'll never know you're operating in it. Our job first is to bring you out of that place of misunderstanding into a place of knowledge so you can gain wisdom. So, you can walk it out when the enemy is still lurking around like a lion seeking whom he may devour. He sees the scar on you too. He sees the wound on you too. But God has a promise in his word and that you're going to be healed.

Healing is a process. If you notice, there were some things in the Bible that were healed instantly and some things that Jesus gave instruction for people to do to obtain healing. So, for people who are always looking for a quick fix, who don't think God will cause you to walk things out, go look in the word. Acts 3:6 says, "Then Peter said, Silver and gold have I none; but such as I have given I thee: In the name of Jesus Christ of Nazareth rise up and walk." You may not think God will require you to partner in faith and works, but James 2:14 says, "Faith without works is dead". We must partner with God to walk in freedom.

Jeremiah tells us that he'll restore us, and restoration is our portion. Health is our portion. Jeremiah was talking about how God

> If you are to believe the truth of the word, then you're listening more to the wound more than you are to the word.

would restore the Israelites because they were an outcast. An outcast is a person who is rejected or excluded, a wanderer, or anything thrown out or rejected, abandoned, or discarded, cast out. A lot of times, wounds cause you to feel abandoned or like an outcast and you don't feel like you fit in anywhere. Everyone has a place in the Kingdom of God. Jesus' mandate was to help people understand that, through the cross, all have been adopted into this Kingdom.

But when you feel abandoned, it often seems like you can't talk to anyone—you feel all alone. You might say, 'Oh, I'm an introvert.' No, you're running from confrontation. Or maybe you say, 'I don't mess with people.' If you've said any of these things, it's time to examine yourself. Leviticus 13:23 talks about how the priest would examine leprosy: 'But if the area grows no larger and does not spread, it is merely the scar from the boil, and the priest will pronounce the person ceremonially clean.' We declare to you that this thing hasn't spread, and you don't have to keep seeing it as something that is spreading and devouring your life. To activate this, I pronounce you ceremonially clean by the blood of the Lamb. You're not stuck in the spirit. The devil will keep trying to hype you up and rehash that memory to make it seem like it is spreading.

If you're struggling to believe the truth of the Word, it may be because you're focusing more on your wounds than on the Word itself. Ask God to help you in your unbelief. When our brothers and sisters in Christ acts as if they believe something they don't, the devil can play games in their minds. If you're pretending to believe something that isn't true, then he has a right to manipulate your thoughts about it. The Bible tells us to resist the devil, and he must flee, right? If you don't resist him, you're simply inviting him in. From the very beginning, God told us that we were made in His image. He was wounded for our transgressions, and we must recognize the significance of this. Being made in His image means we can access the same blood that cleansed and healed us to bring healing to ourselves. Your wounds and scars can become evidence of your Christlikeness in the world. Jesus was wounded and rose from that woundedness to demonstrate that we, too, can walk in liberty. Each of us has been mandated to embrace God's likeness for true freedom. We don't have to remain in bondage.

"I'm amazed when I read about John on Patmos. How do you stay in the Spirit while in exile? How did John remain in such a spiritual realm while in exile and still write the Book of Revelations? I read a book called *God's Generals,* which discusses the old healing evangelists like A.A. Allen, Smith Wigglesworth, and Kathryn Kuhlman. When I got to William Branham, he quoted John and posed a question: How could John stay in the Spirit while in a place of exile to the degree he did? Branham said, 'I had to learn how to stay in the Spirit while walking through and living everyday life.'

Paul teaches us many revelations about those who live in the flesh and die by the flesh, and those who live in the Spirit and walk in the Spirit. We must reach a point where we truly believe we are spirit beings living in fleshly bodies. Our flesh doesn't have to control us; we can control it. We need to grasp the revelation that we are in this world but not of it. We must stick to the script, which is the Word of God. In regard to the Bible, my grandmother Octavia used to say, 'Believe the words you read, not just read the words you believe.'

If you don't get your emotions in check, you'll find yourself on a roller coaster ride of life. During this journey, I realized how much of our lives are tied to our emotions. One moment you're happy, the next you're sad, fearful, angry, or frustrated. All of this is linked to an emotional response. For example, you might say, 'McDonald's was good today,' but if it's bad, you might think, 'I don't want to go back.'

You might feel tired of your job one day and enjoy it the next. All these different emotions are tied to our everyday living. If we, as believers, don't embrace self-control, one of the fruits of the Spirit, we will become emotional wrecks. Within these emotions are two things for sure: a lie and the truth. Whether or not we can discern which is which will dictate the level of freedom we experience. If we can learn to control our emotions and respond wisely to the hurts of life, we give ourselves permission to operate in the peace and power of God.

CLOSING PRAYER

Father God, we come before You with gratitude for everything that has been decreed and declared. We pray that each person receives it in the spirit and comes into Your anointing. You have given us emotions, but we are meant to control them through self-control rather than allowing them to control us. I thank You, Father, that as people pursue their destiny and purpose throughout the day, they will embrace the importance of emotional control. I pray they will not be swept away on the roller coaster ride of emotionalism, but instead navigate life with reason and clarity. Your Word tells us that knowing the truth will set us free. I thank You that they will examine every area of their lives, recognizing that they have been set free and do not have to remain in bondage to past experiences. I pray that every believer, when they look at the wounds and scars in their lives, will be reminded that it took the blood of Jesus to cleanse and heal them. We will forever give You the praise, the glory, and the honor. In Your Son Jesus' name, Amen.

Emotional Me Check-In: How are you Feeling?

Find a quiet space to reflect and invite God into your time of prayer. Use the **Emotional Me Check-In** questionnaire to honestly assess your feelings, their triggers, and any Scripture that speaks to them. Release your emotions to God, seek peace, and consider any actions, like reconciliation or serving others. Reach out for support if needed, and close with gratitude.

1. What am I feeling right now? Can I name this emotion before God?

2. How would I describe this feeling in prayer to God?

3. What does the Bible say about this kind of emotion?

4. How could trusting God impact the way I respond to this emotion?

5. What step can I take to seek peace, healing, or forgiveness in relation to this feeling?

NOTES

Chapter Four

GET UP

> To change your way of thinking you need new information, new principles, and new ideas.

I've said this many times: regardless of how anointed or called you believe you are to ministry, the marketplace, or entrepreneurship, if you cannot manage your thought patterns and live a life of self-control, you will struggle to embrace the fruits of the Spirit. Ultimately, none of your gifts or callings matter if you lack emotional stability. Throughout Scripture, men and women of God have walked into their purpose only to feel a sense of unworthiness or confusion, often allowing past experiences to haunt them. Such feelings can lead us into a state of self-condemnation, where we disqualify ourselves and succumb to a place of emotional turmoil.

Every time someone moves into an emotional realm in the Bible, the Spirit alerts them, or God provokes them through love. It's just a shift, but God does it in multiple ways. Sometimes He speaks to us in an emotional state through love, chastisement, and sternness. God gives us assignments and challenges us to come into alignment with His Word, provoking us with love. He provides understanding through our spiritual leaders, mentors, pastors, and of course our Lord and Savior, Jesus Christ. They teach different principles that challenge our thought patterns, guiding us to conform to the will and Word of God. This concept is captured beautifully in Romans 12:2, which is one of my favorite passages of Scripture: "Do not be conformed to the patterns of this world but be transformed by the renewing of your mind." Essentially, He is saying that to change your way of thinking, you need new information, principles, and ideas. You must establish new laws in your heart that you can grasp and apply to everyday living, leading to real change. As you apply these principles, you will see manifestations of change in your thought patterns.

I was speaking with a woman of God who shared that when she was re-indoctrinated into the new thing and experienced a taste of new wine, her old wine skin had to go because it couldn't hold it. Her old thought patterns had to be discarded because they created conflict. Witnessing the new wine saturating the old wine revealed the truth: the old way was false doctrine; it was a lie. God chastises us to initiate change. He pushes us into assignments or applies pressure to prompt transformation. He teaches us new principles that we can apply to our daily lives for spiritual, physical, and emotional growth.

In this chapter, we will focus on emotional resilience. Last chapter, we discussed wounds and scars. Wounds can cause us to abort our mission. Many times, when we encounter traumatic experiences or are introduced to something entirely new, we may feel wounded due to self-condemnation. God might say, "Hey, I've called you to do this thing, but you have no knowledge of it. You don't know what it is or how to do it." Sometimes, even a God-ordained new thing can feel overwhelming. The lack of knowledge about it can stir up feelings of anxiety and low self-esteem, leading us to question our qualifications: "Why did He call me to this? I don't qualify; I lack the education. I didn't go to seminary. I didn't do this or that." Even good things can lead us into an unhealthy realm of emotionalism that causes wounds.

I am here to declare that what He has called you to, He has already qualified you for. You are fully qualified; you just need to submit to the process of growth required for your journey. There is always a realm of teaching and equipping that accompanies transformation. However, what often happens is that when these thoughts form in our minds, they can cause us to become stagnant. Sometimes, if not all the time, we wouldn't emerge from that place unless we choose to rise up.

I can preach to you, teach you, and prophesy over you, but if you don't receive it, walk it out, and put it into action, you will remain stagnant and never move forward.

OPENING PRAYER

Father, I thank You for what You are doing. I pray that the person reading this will be strengthened and will begin to feel the pulsating flow of blood, the blood that runs from heaven, through Your Son, and into their bodies. Thank You, Father, for breathing a fresh wind of the Holy Spirit into them, empowering them to build the confidence to stand, move forward, and change their perception of their situation. Help them to realize that when You said in Your Word that love never fails, You were not only speaking about loving our brothers and sisters but also about learning to love You and Your principles even more. May that love connection be reciprocated back to You, Lord. We give You the praise, the glory, and the honor. In Jesus' name, Amen.

In Acts 3, the New Living Translation reads: "Peter and John went to the temple one afternoon to take part in the three o'clock prayer service. As they approached the temple, a man lame from birth was being carried in. Each day, he was put beside the temple gate, called the Beautiful Gate, so he could beg from the people going into the temple. When he saw Peter and John, he asked them for some money. Peter and John looked at him intently. Peter said, "Look at us." The lame man looked at them eagerly, expecting some money. But Peter said, "I don't have any silver and gold for you, but I'll give you what I have. In the name of Jesus Christ of Nazareth, get up and walk." Then Peter took the man by the right hand and helped him up. As he did, the man's feet and ankles were instantly healed and strengthened. He jumped up, stood on his feet, began walking, then leaping and praising God. He went into the temple with them. All the people saw him walking and heard him praising God. Reflecting on Peter's words in the King James Version, "Silver and gold I have none, but such as I have give I thee: in the name of Jesus Christ of Nazareth, rise up and walk", we notice a profound shift in the New Living Translation's emphasis on the imperative: "You get up and walk." This distinction reveals not only the healing but also the call to action.

Emotions play a significant role in our cognitive processes, influencing how we perceive, remember, and make judgments. They shape our attention and can motivate both positive and negative behaviors. When we consider the man who was lame from birth, we see a life marred by trauma from the very beginning. He endured a unique set of challenges, unable to walk and often facing societal rejection. One can only imagine how this physical limitation affected his thoughts and feelings throughout his life. Imagine navigating a world where you rely on others for basic needs like getting a cup of water or using the restroom. This man had to humble himself to beg, an act that requires vulnerability many would find difficult. The definition of "beg" implies asking urgently and humbly, highlighting the emotional toll of needing to seek help for every aspect of life. Consider the internal struggle he faced: "Would they understand my plight? Could they empathize with my situation?" His reliance on others for transportation to and from the temple gate likely compounded his feelings of inadequacy and isolation. Living in a constant state of needing assistance, he was conditioned by his circumstances. We often find ourselves in similar situations where trauma limits our behavior. The man was not just physically impaired; he was emotionally and mentally shaped by his lameness. He had learned to navigate life through the lens of his limitations. This indoctrination can mirror our own experiences with pain and hurt, leading us to live by the principles of our wounds.

We might ask ourselves: "Would you carry me because I feel inadequate? Would you pray for me because I feel stuck in my circumstances?" Each question reflects our struggles with shortcomings, disappointments, and the weight of expectations. This story invites us to consider how our emotional traumas can dictate our actions and inhibit our ability to rise up. Just as the lame man had to make the choice to respond to Peter's command, we too must choose to confront our limitations and seek the healing that God offers. In conclusion, the journey from trauma to healing involves recognizing our need for support and the courage to accept help. Just as the man leapt and praised God after his healing, we too can find joy and freedom in our own transformation when we allow God to address the deeper wounds that hold us back.

Most don't even perceive that the gate is beautiful. We only perceive the gate as the place where many people will carry us. They carry us physically, naturally when I hold out my hands. They are carrying me in their hearts and their minds because I indoctrinated them with my lameness to feel pity for me. Could you carry me because I'm always depressed, could you carry me because I'm lost all the time? Could you carry me because the love of money controls me? Could you carry me because I don't understand how to be committed? Could you carry me because I don't understand being celibate? Could you carry me, Lord?

Many of us have operated from a "lame" paradigm. Like the lame man, we often say, "I'm tired, carry me," or "I'm burnt out, carry me." We may not realize that we've been indoctrinated to view life through the lens of our pains and flaws. I was telling someone the other day that when people call me and start with, "I'm tired" or "I'm having a rough day," I'm already planning my exit strategy to get off the phone. What I won't do is accept the impartation of despair, grief, and depression that has jumped on them because they lack the capacity or the will to cast down those vain imaginations. When I make my exit strategy, I might suggest, "Okay, let's meet another time when we can delve deeper into this and possibly seek some deliverance." I'm not going to carry you to the gate in this moment. We've been so conditioned by negative experiences and emotions that our first response to someone asking, "Hi, how are you?" often reflects the struggles of our day. But Nehemiah 8:10 reminds us, "The joy of the Lord is your strength." You may call Him Savior every Sunday, but throughout the week, are you truly living in joy?

Many of you are still asking for permission to overcome challenges that you already have the power to address. You're seeking validation for your existence when all you need to do is stand up and embrace it. The Bible says, "Resist the devil, and he will flee" (James 4:7). We will preach Christ until He comes and crucifies your flesh. We will preach Christ until those emotions are crucified with Him. We will teach these truths until you come into alignment with your identity as a new creation in Christ.

Every day, he sits at the gate, missing out on the possibility of standing up and receiving his healing. Each time he embraces his lameness or asks someone to pacify his situation, he evades the chance for wholeness. Remember, I mentioned that love, chastisement, teaching, and assignment are four ways God transforms us to look more like Him. When someone points out your struggles, it's easy to become defensive. Every time a person offers a word of knowledge about your life, you might feel the urge to dodge their insights, avoiding people who have the grace to help you confront your challenges. You may shy away from the anointing stirring within you, hesitating to bring your struggles to the altar. I notice how some people deflect or evade when confronted; they often want to change the subject instead of addressing the issues at hand.

We sometimes take for granted the transformative power of God, assuming He can't change us or improve our situations. When we lack visible proof of His work in our lives, we may find it hard to believe in our potential for healing and growth. This mindset can lead us to think of life as a series of punishments, reinforcing the belief that we are somehow cursed. Yet, we must remember that faith, even as small as a mustard seed, can move mountains (Matthew 17:20-21). If we can cultivate just a little bit of faith, we will begin to see change manifest in our lives. In time, those mountains will move; we just need to start believing in the possibility of transformation. When someone begs he means to ask to be released from something such as an obligation. Some of you are asking to be free from freedom and liberty. I know what you're asking, but I just can't do that right now." Could you let me do it some other time? Can we do deliverance some other time? Can I come to class some other time? Can we pray another time? Is it okay if I don't show up for prayer today? We've been so conditioned by our past experiences. Can I gain my healing later? Sometimes, I find that I enjoy the attention I get from being carried in and sitting at the gate.

You may have encountered people whom you carry to the gate. They don't realize how much they weigh on you, pulling you down. All they know is that, by indoctrinating you with their lameness, you keep carrying them to the gate. It's so unfortunate that they don't recognize the beauty of the gate, and perhaps you don't either. You keep carrying people who are abusing the grace on your life, taking advantage of your big heart, sympathy, and empathy. They take you for granted, causing you to neglect your own obligations in favor of continuing to carry them. As a result, you can't tap into your dreams or vision because you're so focused on helping them that they've become comfortable relying on you. They may not realize that they can rise up because you won't let them; you keep rushing in to carry them instead.

When you are devoted to prayer, it's not just about showing up on Wednesdays because the apostle and pastor said so. Prayer is your commitment to meet God in that sacred space. Yet, you might skip it because you woke up with a headache, lost your shoe, or didn't set your alarm. When you live your life with purpose, like Peter and John did, you become connected to the source. They were attuned to the source and acted upon its guidance. When Peter and John saw the lame man and told him to get up and walk, they were saying, "Look, you need to take ownership of your situation. Consider that you can pursue your healing and receive the blessings that come with it. Understand that through Christ, you have the power to effect change in your life. You need to cultivate a higher level of thinking and tap into a place where only you and God dwell. Even the word of God tells us to "Make our petition known that you would come into possession of your power" (Philippians 4:6-7 NIV). Your authority as a believer is that you would understand who God says you are. You will be able to withstand the winds and attacks of the enemy, know the enemy and his devices, and that you would come into a realm of God's mindedness, Christ likeness, Christ centered posture, where nothing in your carnal being could control you. do you use your word like you need to?

When Jesus was in the wilderness tempted and attacked by the enemy, he used the word. He didn't profess, confess, decree, or declare the lameness. Some of us are offended by people pointing out the fact that we just need to come all up. We just need to step up. Peter isn't so much telling him to stand up first, he's giving a command that he has to first receive in his mind before his center could ever begin the process of speaking to the nervous system and moving down to his feet. He says get up. He says, first I need you to walk in my authority as I command you to get up. You're sitting at the temple where God lives, you're sitting at the gate called beautiful. I must tell you where you are and remind you to get up. Stop talking like you think when you have a bigger mindset.

I just told you in my intro that your emotions can affect your mental process of perception. I just told you that ultimately evil perception will also affect your ability to act how you behave. He says, I must command you to embrace a God like behavior so that you will no longer evade your healing. I must release the command to you to come up higher in your thinking. To do the work, you must perceive first in your mind. Sometimes that takes pointing out the truth that you're operating from a carnal demonic paradigm. You indoctrinate yourself with your deficiencies. You define yourself by your lameness. then you intrude on others' lives with your lameness by placing false expectations on them to carry you when all you must do is get up.

Peter said, "I don't have the things you're asking everyone else for. I'm not going to drop a coin in your cup, and I'm not going to carry you. I won't pay you to keep sitting at the gate or to remain in your current state. I refuse to support you in staying sick or continuing to view yourself in a negative light. I won't allow you to dwell in loneliness and despair. I won't let you sit at that gate and complain about your job when God has provided for you. I'm not going to keep placing bandages on your thinking, as if operating from a place of inferiority is acceptable. I won't just say, 'It's going to be alright; just trust God,' while continuing to enable the very mindset that holds you back. This mindset is harmful because it can lead you to desire it over your healing and over the truth of who God is. Peter made it clear: "I'm not going to pay you to stay in low self-esteem and self-condemnation. I won't carry you back into that state."

After we've prophesied, after the intercessors have prayed, and after we've cast out the demons operating in your life, you still have to commit to walking out your deliverance. The memory of your past experiences may linger. I can cast out that demon, but you can still hold onto the pain. I can remove that demonic spirit, yet you may still embrace your circumstances. So, I'm not going to keep dropping coins into your cup. I'm reminded of my trips home to New Orleans, where I've seen musicians playing "When the Saints Go Marching In" while people drop dollars into their cups. That's how we often sit at the gate singing our tune of, "I'm hurt, I'm broken, I'm emotionally distressed. Could you please pay me to stay this way?" It's crucial to recognize where you are sitting, as many of us fail to understand the significance of our position.

If we look up the word "gate," we see it defined as a door used for any opening, like a passage into a tomb (thefreedictionary.com). The man is sitting at a gate that represents a rite of passage into healing. He's positioned where God's people come to worship, a place where priests, prophets, and apostles gather. He's at the gate of authority. Another definition of a gate is an open door that signifies the opportunity to do something (thefreedictionary.com). He is sitting at the gate where transformative events can occur. Furthermore, it signifies the door to the Kingdom of Heaven, indicating the conditions that must be met to be received into the Kingdom of God.

He's sitting at a pathway that could lead him to becoming a Kingdom man. As sons and daughters of God, we are heirs of salvation, which grants us the right of passage as children of the gatekeeper. We always have access. That's why Paul said, "The spirit is willing, but the flesh is weak." The spirit desires to go through the gate, while the flesh wants to remain seated at it. This man is positioned at the gate that could provide access to new opportunities and the Kingdom of God. However, he has become so indoctrinated by his past experiences that he lacks the capacity to recognize that he is at the threshold of healing.

Many of us are sitting right at the gate, yet we don't perceive its significance. God is offering you deliverance through four means: love, chastisement, assignment, and teaching. Some of you have received love in various forms to guide you toward healing and wholeness. Perhaps God has been correcting your thought patterns, desiring that you be transformed by the renewing of your mind.

God has also been giving you new assignments, knowing that something along that journey will change the way you see yourself. Consider Peter: Jesus said, "Follow me, and I will make you fishers of men" (Matthew 4:19). Even at the Last Supper, Jesus predicted Peter's denial, saying he would deny Him three times. This revelation deepened Peter's love for God when he repented. You might find yourself on an assignment that leads you to a place of repentance. Your assignment is foundational to the Kingdom, and through it, God is giving you keys to the Kingdom and the authority needed to overcome your own limitations.

God has placed you among people who teach according to Kingdom principles, guiding you toward true healing and transformation. Their teachings have been taking root in your heart and mind, reshaping your emotions and fostering a metamorphosis as you embrace this new theology and apply it to your life. As you make the Word a habit, you'll learn to walk in Christlikeness. You rise up and step into the higher position that God has been calling you to occupy. You receive what He has been drawing you toward, pursuing it with the faith to obtain it because someone has taught you, loved you, and corrected you enough to inspire that journey. God has given you the assignment that will empower you to get up!

Beautiful" is defined as blooming and describes that which is seasonable produced at the right time, like the prime of life or the moment when anything is at its loveliest and best. The man is sitting at the Beautiful Gate, a place where things bloom at the right time and appear at their finest. He may not realize that the name of this gate prophetically signifies that he is at the open door to the Kingdom. This is the moment for him to bloom: his feet will stir, his ankles will strengthen, and he will be transformed into a sight of beauty as he runs down the street. People will look at him and say, "Don't they look their best today? This is the best I've ever seen them!" God has touched their life at the gate. Peter and John were going to the temple to pray, fully aware that walking through the Beautiful Gate meant that the things they prayed for would inevitably bloom and manifest. The petals of possibility begin to open, and the fruit of their faith starts to grow.

When you sense the call to pray, the kind of prayer that stirs change, show up. Even if you don't see it immediately, know that things are happening in the spiritual realm. Things are being birthed. Manifestations are on the horizon. Remember the story of the gate called Beautiful—a place of transformation, where divine timing aligns.

God is sitting at this gate, a place where things bloom, unfold, and align perfectly in His time. Peter and John, apostles of new beginnings, went to this gate, and in doing so, they became vessels of breakthrough for a lame man. They didn't give him coins, but instead, they offered a greater grace: the ability to pioneer something new. This is Kingdom grace at work—a gift to usher in transformation.

Notice how, in Acts 3:4, Peter and John looked at the lame man intently and said, "Look at us." They needed his attention; they needed him to shift his focus from his usual expectations to something divine. They wanted him to see what God was doing. Many of us are in that "look at us" moment where God is trying to get our attention. Maybe it's in your career, a relationship, a transition, or a Kingdom assignment. God is calling us to lift our eyes from what we're used to and to discern what He's birthing.

Consider the story of Elisha and Elijah. Elisha wanted the mantle, and Elijah told him, "If you see me when I'm taken, it will be yours." It required discernment, a focused attention on the divine moment. Similarly, Peter and John knew that timing and discernment are key to experiencing Kingdom breakthroughs. If we stay locked in an old mindset, we risk missing the moment when things bloom, when God's timing and purpose align.

The gate is called Beautiful for a reason—it's the blooming place, the moment where things come into fullness. In this season, let's position ourselves to discern and respond, to see the opportunities God is unfolding. It's time to see, to look up, and recognize the "gate called Beautiful" moments God is inviting us into.

The gate is called Beautiful—a place where things bloom and come into their best form. It represents divine timing, where things are made lovely and display their full potential. Peter and John told the man at this gate, "Look at us," because they were about to make a declaration over his life that would change him. From that moment, others would see him and recognize the transformation brought by the Kingdom.

As I mentioned earlier, Peter and John had to tell him to get up. His emotions and the weight of his condition had impacted his mindset, making it hard for him to see beyond his limitations. God desires to shape our actions and behaviors to reflect His will and purpose. That's why He calls us to submit our lives as a living sacrifice, holy and pleasing to His Word and His will.

When we allow unhealthy emotions to control us, they can stifle us, rendering us "lame" in our spiritual walk. They hinder us from moving forward in God's purpose, keeping us sitting at the gate instead of rising up in His strength. But just as Peter and John's words stirred the lame man to get up, God's Word is calling us to stand and walk into the fullness of His purpose, leaving behind anything that keeps us "stuck" at the gate.

> **We often miss what God is doing because we're focused and influenced by our past pain**

Too often, we find ourselves sitting at the gate called anxiety because we don't discern the potential beauty beyond it. We stay at the gate of depression because we haven't decided to see the possibilities God has placed there. We sit at the gate, speaking about our loneliness, unaware that this very place could give us access to a new realm of God's presence. We sit at the gate, declaring our low self-esteem and rehearsing everything we've been through, unable to see that God is inviting us to stand up and walk forward. What if we saw each of these gates as places of transition rather than destinations? God is calling us to discern that the "gate" is not our final stop—it's a threshold into transformation. At these gates, He invites us to see what He can make beautiful, and to step beyond what's holding us back.

We sit at the gate, speaking of things like divorce, unaware that we're actually at a place of transformation—a gate that could bring about a metamorphosis. But we often miss what God is doing because we're so focused and influenced by our past pain, unable to see beyond it. This fixation renders us spiritually "lame," stuck without movement, and begging without hope for change. God invites us to look up, to discern His hand at work, and to rise beyond what we've been through into the new life He's calling us toward.

Peter and John invited the lame man to rise to a higher place with God. They told him, "You're sitting at an open door of access, and

God sent us to help you. We won't cater to your lameness, but we will confront it at the root and cast it out." They reminded him that he had to partner with them in faith because, as James 2:17 says, *"faith without works is dead."* The man had focused more on his limitations than on his faith, but God was calling him back to life. As the story continues, the man took a step, and Peter reached out to help him the rest of the way. This wasn't just authority at work—it was love. Though Peter and John spoke with boldness, it was love that compelled them to pull him up from the gate. They saw that he kept sitting there, unaware that all he needed to do was stand up. God wants you to know you, too, can get up.

Every day, declare that you're going to rise. Stop speaking about your "lameness" or limitations and start declaring, *"I can do all things through Christ who strengthens me"* (Philippians 4:13). Make this your declaration. Even science tells us that if you repeat an action for 28 to 30 days, it can become a habit. So, commit to getting up for 30 days straight. Don't let how you feel in the natural hold you back, and don't impose that mindset on others. When people ask how you're doing, you don't have to dwell on what's wrong—choose to speak life instead. God hasn't called you to be a pessimistic believer. Being pessimistic is living by the flesh; God calls you to live in hope and faith.

Here's a clearer, more concise version of the message:

Make positivity a habit. As I mentioned earlier, when others bring negativity into your life, you don't have to sit and absorb it. I'll say, "I love you, but I have to go," and hang up. Then, I denounce every bit of negativity and move on. Start embracing the ways God uses to help you grow and mature.

God chastises those He loves. Stop avoiding people who correct you in love; their guidance can lead to real change. Much of my growth came from no longer taking offense when someone encouraged me to improve. True personal and spiritual growth flourishes when we can receive constructive criticism, not confuse it with judgment. Some people miss out on growth because they label everything as judgment. I reject that mindset and pray you will see constructive criticism for what it is. Look at Scripture: when the prophet Nathan confronted David or when Samuel corrected Saul, they were motivated by love and God's truth. Jesus Himself showed love through correction, often saying, *"O faithless generation, how long shall I be with you?"* (Matthew 17:17). Jesus loves us enough to correct us, knowing that true love sometimes means challenging us to do better. Embrace correction—it's a gift that leads to maturity.

In Hebrews 5:12, Paul challenges believers, saying, *"By this time you ought to be teachers, yet you still need someone to teach you the basics of God's word. You're like babies who need milk instead of solid food"* (NLT). Verses 13-14 go on to say, *"Anyone who lives on milk is still an infant and doesn't know how to do what is right. Solid food is for those who are mature, who through training have the skill to recognize the difference between right and wrong."* This passage reminds us that we can't grow if we keep running from constructive criticism. How do we tell the difference between judgment and constructive criticism? Look for love. Ask yourself: *Does this person genuinely care about me? Do I know they're speaking to help me, not to hurt me?* When we understand that someone's correction is rooted in love, we can receive it as wisdom and growth, not as criticism. Instead of running from those who care about your growth, lean into what they're saying. They're likely dropping wisdom that can change your life. It's also essential to sit under sound, balanced teaching that provides guidance and maturity. Embrace the "solid food" of God's wisdom and move beyond the basics to deeper understanding and growth.

A minister who understands spiritual gifts goes beyond theological training; according to Amos 3:7, they also reveal God's secrets. There are mysteries within God's Word that only a prophetic voice can unveil. As the Scripture states, *"Surely the Lord God does nothing unless He reveals His secret to His servants the prophets."* Prophetic insight is essential for uncovering truths that may not be immediately apparent. This was why the Pharisees and Sadducees didn't understand the mystery that Gentiles would be included in God's family; their focus was on tradition, denominationalism, and religion, not a genuine relationship with God. We need prophetic voices who can declare the Word, make it clear, and break down complex truths. Understanding the written Word requires context, but drawing out its deeper secrets requires revelation.

Paul followed tradition throughout his life until he encountered a profound revelation on the road to Damascus. It was there that he truly heard and communicated with God, who asked him, *"Why are you persecuting me?"* Although Paul was well-versed in Scripture, he had been killing Christians based on the theological perspective of the high priest. Through this revelation, he recognized how he had been indoctrinated and misguided. To grow in understanding, you need a teacher—not just someone with a seminary education, but a teacher who is revelatory, practical, and prophetically insightful. Such a teacher can help reconcile confusion. Remember, your emotions influence how you think, process information, perceive situations, make judgments, and reason through issues. A good teacher can bring all of that back to truth. You need God's love and the right assignment, along with His revelation of the mysteries of the gospel. It's essential to have a prophetic voice that can clarify truths about yourself that you may not yet understand. God is calling you to rise above your emotional struggles and step into the fullness of His purpose for your life.

CLOSING PRAYER

Father, I thank You for loving Your body of believers. I thank You, Father God, that someone's legs and ankles are being strengthened because we have declared to them that they can get up. Someone's legs, joints, limbs, muscles, and bones are gaining strength and nutrients to enable them to stand. We have called them out and told them to look at You, to perceive who You are and what You can do.

Father, I thank You that a baby has been birthed. Someone is about to give birth. I thank You that someone's life is being transformed. I thank You that they are entering into a realm of self-control, in accordance with the fruits of the Holy Spirit as stated in Galatians 5:22-23, that they would embrace this realm of self-control. I thank You that someone will no longer consider themselves lame; instead, they will discern that they are at the gate called Beautiful—the blooming place, the place of right timing. They are at the gate, the access point to the Kingdom, the open door, and they are about to walk through it.

I thank You, Father, that according to this passage, after the lame man was healed, he went running and shouting through the city, and everyone knew and could perceive that he had been changed. I thank You that this chapter is not just about healing but also about the transformation of those around them. I thank You that someone will no longer enable others' lameness; instead, they will challenge their own limits with truth. I pray that they will perceive and receive constructive criticism and discern that those who have authority come in love to speak truth to the powers operating in their lives. The only power that can resonate is the Kingdom. We give You the praise, the glory, and the honor. Amen, and get up!

Emotional Me Check-In: How are you Feeling?

Find a quiet space to reflect and invite God into your time of prayer. Use the **Emotional Me Check-In** questionnaire to honestly assess your feelings, their triggers, and any Scripture that speaks to them. Release your emotions to God, seek peace, and consider any actions, like reconciliation or serving others. Reach out for support if needed, and close with gratitude.

1. What am I feeling right now? Can I name this emotion before God?

2. How would I describe this feeling in prayer to God?

3. What does the Bible say about this kind of emotion?

4. How could trusting God impact the way I respond to this emotion?

5. What step can I take to seek peace, healing, or forgiveness in relation to this feeling?

NOTES

Chapter Five

WONDERFUL COUNSELOR

Activate School of Ministry was inspired by the passage where Paul encourages us to remember to stir up the gift within us (see 2 Timothy 1:6). While studying this passage, the Lord led me to the dictionary, where I found that "stir" is defined as "to cause to become active." Paul speaks of gifts, which represent our identity as Christians and our ability to operate in our God-given gifts. These gifts are examples and expressions of God's nature. When Paul urges us to stir up God's nature within us, he is calling us to activate that divine essence. My heart's desire is to help you activate the nature of God that is already within you. At the very start of creation, God declared that we are made in His image and likeness, indicating that there are divine qualities within you.

I pray that the God-likeness within you is stirred and comes alive. I encourage you to enter a realm where you actively operate in and apply the Word and will of God in your life. This will empower you to manifest eternity and bring the heavens to Earth.

As Jesus taught us to pray, "Thy will be done on earth as it is in heaven." My desire is that each time you read this book, you experience an activation of godly principles in your life, so that you become more like Christ. This is the essence of being a Christian. Often, we forget that our daily walk should reflect Christ-likeness. Our mandate as believers, empowered by the Holy Spirit, is not to be like anyone else, but to be like Christ.

> Many have been taught the Word in-depth but still struggle to apply it.

As we dive into God's Word, we should see more of Christ imparted into us and flowing through us. Each day, we should witness Christ's likeness manifesting as we shed our old selves and embrace the new creation, we are in Him. We cannot remain unchanged. We must stop allowing our past experiences to define us. I believe God is calling us to rise above a mindset of offense and defense, which often leads to the excuse, "Well, that's just who I am." God is saying, "That is not who I have called you to be. I am calling you to embody My likeness."

We've been discussing the topic of emotions from a biblical perspective. The Lord has been revealing different scriptures to me in this season. No matter who you are or what you are called to do, your emotions impact everything. They affect your mind, will, and emotions, as well as your physical, mental, and spiritual well-being. They influence everything you need to function in everyday life. If you struggle to function daily, it will be even more difficult to operate in the Kingdom, where there are mandates and requirements.

You may not have fully benefited from what God can do in your life because you haven't learned these simple principles. Please hear me when I say "learn." I mean learning to apply these principles in your life. Many of us have become spiritually overweight from being fed the Word, yet we have not learned to apply it outside of manipulation. Many have been taught the Word in-depth but still struggle to apply it. What good does it do if we teach, and you can't apply? What good does it do if we preach, and you still can't live it? If we hope and you are still lost, we haven't done our job.

I believe God is raising up a generation of leaders who thrive because they are emotionally healthy. They succeed because they have truly learned the application of these principles in their own lives. You can't teach what you haven't learned. We have focused on knowledge and information but often neglect the application. As a result, many leaders have become burnt out, witnessing a cycle of people in the body of Christ who repeatedly deal with the same issues. If they had learned the application, they would be able to shift and transform.

In this season, I believe God is raising up people who will first take on the mind of Christ and embrace these principles so that they can then impart them to others.

I've been discussing emotions through the lens of various revelations that God has placed in my spirit. We began by laying a foundation of wounds and scars. Then we discussed the warfare of emotions. In the last chapter, we focused on "Get Up." In this chapter, we will explore "Wonderful Counselor." We'll be looking at Isaiah 9:6, but verses 1-7 will help us establish the foundation.

OPENING PRAYER

Father God, I thank You for being here with us tonight. I thank You that You love us and desire for us to be whole. I appreciate that You want us to reject and rid ourselves of the false thinking we have embraced through years of wrong teaching and doctrine. I thank You, Father, for helping us overcome the negative experiences and moments of trauma and despair that have indoctrinated us into bad thinking and distorted perceptions. I thank You tonight that You will do what You desire to do. Equip Your people, activate them, and stir them up so they can walk in freedom. Open the doors that they may see and walk into the marvelous light that You are. Father, I thank You for bringing them out of darkness into Your marvelous light. I praise You, Father, for calling them up higher. In Jesus' name, Amen. Thank You, Lord.

Isaiah 9:1-7 in the New Living Translation says: "Nevertheless, that time of darkness and despair will not go on forever. The land of Zebulun and Naphtali will be humbled, but there will be a time in the future when Galilee of the Gentiles, which lies along the road that runs between the Jordan and the sea, will be filled with glory.

The people who walk in darkness will see a great light. For those who live in a land of deep darkness, a light will shine. You will enlarge the nation of Israel, and its people will rejoice. They will rejoice before you as people rejoice at the harvest and like warriors dividing the plunder.

For you will break the yoke of their slavery and lift the heavy burden from their shoulders. You will break the oppressor's rod, just as you did when you destroyed the army of Midian. The boots of the warrior and the uniforms bloodstained by war will all be burned. They will be fuel for the fire.

For a child is born to us, a son is given to us. The government will rest on his shoulders. And he will be called: Wonderful Counselor, Mighty God, Everlasting Father, Prince of Peace. His government and its peace will never end. He will rule with fairness and justice from the throne of his ancestor David for all eternity. The passionate commitment of the LORD of Heaven's Armies will make this happen!"

Here, we see the prophecy from the prophet Isaiah, foretelling the coming of the Messiah. In this prophecy, he is painting a picture of how our Savior will restore Israel and reconcile the people back to God. Isaiah is prophesying our Savior's mandate, showing us what He will do when He arrives. We get the title "Wonderful Counselor" because often we don't realize that Jesus is God in the flesh. As leaders and believers, we are called to be created in His likeness, becoming "wonderful counselors" to those who encounter us.

There are two realms: the natural realm, where God has made us in His image, and the realm of counsel, where we are called to support and help one another. The Bible instructs us to bear one another's burdens. Likewise, we should also be bold enough to seek counsel ourselves—from both God and godly people.

For too long, the church has sometimes discouraged people from seeking real help, using well-meaning but ineffective clichés. Because we've viewed people's situations through a natural perspective rather than a Kingdom or compassionate response, we've often turned them away with phrases like, "Just trust God," "Be strong and stand up for yourself," or "You don't need to tell all your business." In some communities, people have stigmatized counseling, making it seem unnecessary or labeling people as "crazy" for seeking help. Yet, God Himself is called the "Wonderful Counselor," and it was prophesied that He would be this for us.

When you've been dismissed or turned away with clichés like "just trust God," it's hard to know what that really means or how to apply it when you're struggling. How do you apply "trust God" when you're facing overwhelming pain? How do you press toward the mark of a higher calling in moments of despair? Without practical guidance, believers have sometimes felt forced to mask their struggles with a false sense of boldness and strength while bleeding internally. Inside, they carry wounds that have only scabbed over without true healing. These wounds hold layers of trauma, pain, and unresolved hurts. Instead of receiving the help they need, many are left with misguided teachings about the Gospel and who God truly is, which do little to soothe their struggles. We need to provide real application and support for the Word in people's lives, so they can find true healing and transformation.

Since we often don't know how to apply the Word, we end up cloaking ourselves in clichés, quoting verses like, "If I wait on the Lord, He will renew my strength and I will mount up on wings like eagles"

(Isaiah 40:31), without understanding how to live it out. Or we say, "If I just confess with my mouth and believe in my heart," not realizing that our hearts are filled with turmoil. We might even quote Hebrews 11:1, "Now faith is the substance of things hoped for, the evidence of things not seen," but struggle to understand what faith really means in our circumstances. So many of us have been manipulated or taught in error, to the point that we talk about having faith the size of a mustard seed, yet lack real faith, insight, perspective, and understanding. How, then, do we believe for healing? How do we believe for deliverance? We keep reproducing these shallow phrases, and now everyone is quoting clichés that don't truly help. So how can I bear the burdens of my brother if I don't even know how to help?

If I try to encourage you by saying, "God's got it," how can you move forward or place that weight on Him when you're still struggling to believe in God, let alone trust Him with your situation? By doing this, we've scattered the sheep, sending them off to graze alone without the nourishment and protection of the Father, who is the true Counselor. They've been left to learn to guide themselves. The danger here is like allowing children to make decisions they're not ready for; we know they lack the understanding that comes with maturity. Yet, we sometimes attempt to handle things ourselves, even when we don't have the capacity. That's why we need the Father and need to see Him as our Wonderful Counselor. God comes to guide us, to realign us with His will, and to help us find true support and direction.

Here, we see that Isaiah prophesied the coming of the Savior. Let's go back to verse six: "For a child is born to us, a son is given to us." First, we need to understand that He was given to us. If we don't know why God sent Jesus to us, how to relate to Him, or what His role is in our lives, then when emotional trauma stirs, we won't go to Him. He was devoted, consecrated, dedicated, given over, delivered up, and

> The old ways taught us to mask so much that we're left only with a mask.

assigned to us. The Son was sent specifically for us—His whole assignment was us. Receive that revelation: *you are God's assignment.* Jesus came to earth for us, and even after His death, resurrection, and ascension, He remains devoted to us. Scripture says He is seated at the right hand of the Father, interceding for us. He is entrusted with our lives. Verse six continues, "and the government will rest on his shoulders." In this passage, "government" refers to rule or dominion. Just as we are called to take dominion over the earth, His assignment is to take dominion and rule over our lives.

Have you given Him that space? That's why John 3:16 says, "if you believe." Believing implies that we must come into agreement with Him before He will take dominion. We must agree with His principles, practice them, and apply them in our lives for Him to have full rule over us. God's purpose is to take dominion over everything operating in our lives. This passage says "the government will rest on His shoulders"—signifying that He will carry our burdens. When we allow Him dominion over our lives, He shoulders the weight for us.

Shoulders represent a place of burden. His shoulders metaphorically signify that God is willing to carry those burdens for you, but you must willingly hand them over. He knows, He is concerned, and He cares for you. You must consent to take His yoke upon you, for His yoke is easy, and His burden is light. You must agree to give Him all of it, casting every care on Him. This is a consent-based relationship where you say, "God, I hand over everything inside me; I give You dominion over my anger, my pain, my fears." You release it because you recognize you can't carry it in your own strength. You've masked it, hidden it, tried to play it off as though you're okay, but inside there is turmoil and torment. The old ways taught us to mask so much that we're left only with a mask. We've been taught to hide it so deeply that we're afraid to speak up, afraid to be vulnerable, because we were once turned away. But not today. Today, I consent. Today, I hand it all over to You, God.

Now, remember that "shoulder" is defined as the place of burden, and a "burden" is something that is emotionally too difficult to bear. Who would have thought that Isaiah prophesied God would come in the flesh through His Son, Jesus, to bear all our emotional despair? Why did He come? Because He understands that emotions can lead us to act irrationally. I've talked about how emotions can cause us to think, act, and respond without reason. They can lead us to behave ignorantly or harbor unforgiveness. Isaiah says, "And the government will rest on His shoulders." The dominion over your emotions will be judged as you allow the Messiah to carry them for you.

Even in a natural setting, when you go to see a counselor, one of the first things you have to sign is a consent form. This is a trust agreement that signifies you trust the counselor to help carry the weight of your burdens. Do you trust God enough to hand Him your struggles so He can judge them? Do you trust Him enough to open up and let Him take your mess? Are you willing to give Him your unforgiveness and trauma? Some of us like to hold on to our issues because they become excuses for acting out of character. They serve as a crutch. We may think, "I can't stop my negative behavior, because if I get delivered and set free, I'll be accountable for my actions." I must now find a healthy way to relate to others, so I can draw the right kind of attention.

The King James Version states, "His name will be called." Meaning His reputation will be that of a Wonderful Counselor, Mighty God, Everlasting Father, and Prince of Peace. These titles represent His characteristics and traits. In other words, if you place your burdens on His shoulders and allow Him to have dominion over your emotions and thoughts, you will experience the Wonderful Counselor, the Mighty God, the Everlasting Father, and the Prince of Peace. The term

"Wonderful" is defined as something extraordinary. When God goes to work, and the Wonderful Counselor comes to guide you, you may not always understand how He counsels you. You might not grasp His advice or instructions, nor comprehend why He does things a certain way. However, you can trust that whatever He does will be extraordinary.

The Wonderful Counselor comes not only to be extraordinary, but He also articulates His purpose in ways that you may not fully understand. The core goal is to judge what has been operating falsely in your life so that you can maintain redemption. He seeks to reconcile and redeem all the negative thoughts that arose from emotions linked to experiences that were introduced in an illegal manner. I hope you're catching that. Many of us are uncomfortable when we hear the word "judgment." When we say that God is judging a situation, it's important to understand that judgment precedes redemption. Judgment is defined as the act or process of forming an opinion after careful consideration or deliberation; it involves the mental ability to perceive and distinguish (TheFreeDictionary.com). God comes to deliberate on what is happening and to decide how to address it.

Judgment is also defined as a determination made by a court of law. Therefore, when He speaks of being "wonderful," He does so through the lens of legal authority. This perspective aligns with what Paul says in Ephesians 6:12 (KJV): "For we wrestle not against flesh and blood, but against powers, against principalities, against the rulers of the darkness of this world, and against spiritual wickedness in high places." The enemy seeks to impose principles through principalities, which manifest as negative experiences. These experiences occur because the enemy tries to establish erroneous principles or laws that disrupt your life. Such disruptions can infiltrate the fruits that God intended to emerge from you, affecting your character and ultimately creating a rift between you and God. When God comes to judge a situation, He is redeeming the principles that have fallen out of alignment so that you can function within a kingdom framework.

The fruits of the Spirit align with God's principles and commandments—not just the Ten Commandments, but also the promises He has spoken over your life, as outlined in biblical doctrine. David said, "Your word I have hidden in my heart, that I might not sin against You" (Psalm 119:11 KJV). He was referring to these principles, expressing that he has committed his life to God's laws so that erroneous principles or principalities have no authority in his life. The Wonderful Counselor hears our hearts and judges those matters. When we discuss judgment in the life of a believer, we are not implying that God is coming to condemn you to hell. Instead, He is here to judge the erroneous or illegal systems that operate in your life—systems that have infiltrated your heart through traumatic experiences—so that He can redeem you back to a right standing with the Father.

God seeks to redeem and judge your emotional state so that you can function from a healthy, biblical paradigm. This approach prevents you from acting solely on desire and selfishness and allows you to operate from a love-centered perspective. It begins with loving God enough to relinquish the burdens you hold hostage.

The definition of a counselor is to advise and consult. We need to consult God more often, meaning He wants us to give Him our burdens and tell Him about our struggles. He cannot do anything with the issues that we refuse to share with Him. Our emotions can become strongholds, leading to bondage and torment. According to The Free Dictionary, a counselor is a person—especially a licensed professional—who treats individuals with mental, emotional, and behavioral disorders and problems. God comes to judge and address our mental, emotional, and behavioral issues, helping us return to a right standing with Him. We must place the burdens and emotions that have become too difficult to bear on His shoulders. Too often, we carry things that we were never meant to bear.

We often see people going to the gym, striving to achieve impressive physiques. While they may appear strong on the outside, how many of them can mentally carry that weight? We tend to focus on building an outward appearance rather than addressing what lies within. This is where the message of discernment comes in. Mature believers are called to recognize when something is operating illegally in their lives. We must have the boldness and courage to stand firm in our faith. A warrior is defined as a champion, and God wants to demonstrate that He can be a warrior in our lives. He wants to show us that He can be a champion, defeating the challenges we face. The Scripture describes Him as a strong man, brave and mighty in nature. The term "mighty" is defined as powerful by implication, highlighting His ability to support and strengthen us.

It's in His nature to be a warrior, a champion. He is strong and brave on your behalf. He is your champion because He is destined to win. God is defined as our hero. He wants you to know that you can trust Him as your hero. I believe all of this is prophetic, particularly in the order it is presented in Scripture. He begins by stating that He must be a Wonderful Counselor. Essentially, He is coming to judge—everything that operates illegally will be judged, and then you will be redeemed. He will provide you with counsel so that you can fulfill your godly assignment. In that moment, He will prove that He is mighty and a champion. As you press in and move forward, because you have placed your burdens on His shoulders, He will fight for you, not the other way around.

We often find ourselves fighting against people, embracing negative thoughts, and walking in self-condemnation when we should be fighting the devil instead. God has declared that all we need to do is resist the devil. Scripture tells us to resist him, and he will flee (James

4:7 KJV). Why will he flee? Because when you resist him, you are handing your burdens over to God, who will bear them on His shoulders and fight for you. When you proclaim, "You shall hold your peace," He will fight for you. I love how Exodus 14:14 reads in The Message Bible: "God will fight the battle for you. And you? You keep your mouths shut!" It is in His nature to be a warrior, a champion, and a hero. He is referred to as the Mighty God. Then He is also called the Everlasting Father. "Everlasting" is defined as continuous existence, extending into the future.

Even as He fights and wars for you, He will be your warrior and champion. When you place your burdens on His shoulders, both now and in times to come, He'll fight for you continually. He is the Everlasting Father. A father is defined as a producer, a generator; as such, He will produce in your life both now and in the future. God is our Father, and in this role, He calls us into relationship. This relationship allows Him to operate as a warrior on your behalf. Why? Because He is truly your Father. What He demonstrates as a warrior is His rightful, legal access—access that you grant Him. He is willing to operate as "Daddy," but He waits for you to ask. Just as He said, place it on His shoulder. He won't step in until you acknowledge your need and give Him permission. He also says He is the Prince of Peace. "Prince" is defined as captain, general, or commander of the military. Isaiah, in this realm, was prophesying a commander, a warrior, a general, a captain whose mission is to go to war on your behalf—so that your mental, emotional, and behavioral struggles may be aligned, judged, and redeemed. Your sins, traumas, and even the sins of others that affected your life have left wounds, but you don't need to remain a victim. When you know Him as a Wonderful Counselor, the One who comes to judge and deliberate your issues, you understand that He takes dominion over your trauma. He is the Captain, the General, the Commander of Peace.

"Peace" is defined as completeness, soundness, welfare, safety, health, prosperity, quietness, tranquility, contentment, peace in friendships, and healthy relationships. In your covenant relationship with God, He wants you to place everything on His shoulders so that you can experience true peace. This allows you to walk in a realm of peace—soundness of thought, understanding, and safety—knowing He will protect you. Paul said, "Whatever state I'm in, I will be content." With this perspective, nothing should stir an emotional reaction in you. When you truly release your burdens and give them to God, anxiety and stress should no longer dominate your response.

God desires for you to walk in peace within your covenant relationship with Him. He wants you to experience peace in your earthly life and to be prepared for the peace of eternity. God intends for you to carry out His purposes, but first, you must see Him as the Wonderful Counselor. Allow Him to carry the burdens that are too heavy for you, so you can walk in wholeness, free from conflict with people, situations, or challenges.

Sometimes, warfare comes through the lens of people, places, and things. But our focus shouldn't be on who or what the enemy uses; it should be on God. The people and circumstances are often disguises meant to distract us, so we focus on them instead of recognizing the enemy at work. Sometimes, it's ourselves we need to examine. Sometimes, it's the place or the timing. Ultimately, God wants us to get to the root of the issue—the enemy's illegal operation in our lives, seeking to undermine God's love for us and His work in us.

When we don't surrender these burdens to God and allow Him to judge them, we may begin acting destructively. Without His intervention, we risk damaging our relationships and our personal lives. Be bold enough to seek God's counsel and lean on the trustworthy people He's placed in your life. He is the Wonderful Counselor, as

Isaiah prophesied, who invites us to place the burdens and emotions too heavy to bear onto His shoulders.

God wants us to embrace the fruits of the Spirit. You will be guided by one of two things: the Spirit or your flesh—both of which engage with your emotions. The difference is that the enemy uses your emotions to tear you down, while the Holy Spirit guides you to express them in a healthy way, allowing you to process them with truth and reason, bringing glory to God in your life. This way, you walk in peace and wholeness, preserving your relationships with God and others, and becoming a conduit of His love on earth. He is our Wonderful Counselor, guiding us to rise above our emotions.

CLOSING PRAYER

Father, I thank You that this chapter allows us to place the weight of our burdens, emotions, experiences, and trauma on Your shoulders so that You can judge them and redeem us. I thank You, Father, that boldness will arise in these believers because You have promised to be the Prince of Peace in our lives. As we surrender our burdens to You, You will use Your authority to bring us into completeness and wholeness in our relationships—with You, with others, and in every area of our lives. Father God, we thank You, and we declare double portions of blessings, favor, and honor over them. In Jesus' name, Amen.

Emotional Me Check-In: How are you Feeling?

Find a quiet space to reflect and invite God into your time of prayer. Use the **Emotional Me Check-In** questionnaire to honestly assess your feelings, their triggers, and any Scripture that speaks to them. Release your emotions to God, seek peace, and consider any actions, like reconciliation or serving others. Reach out for support if needed, and close with gratitude.

1. What am I feeling right now? Can I name this emotion before God?

2. How would I describe this feeling in prayer to God?

3. What does the Bible say about this kind of emotion?

4. How could trusting God impact the way I respond to this emotion?

5. What step can I take to seek peace, healing, or forgiveness in relation to this feeling?

NOTES

Chapter Six

EMOTIONAL TRIGGERS

In the church, we see a lot of emotionalisms, where everything seems tied to being moved emotionally. Many churches have adopted tactics similar to those of the world, using subliminal messages and marketing strategies to attract people. Emotionalism has become a tool to draw individuals in, leading to the rise of various online ministry marketing, coaching, and mentoring programs. For example, we have online courses, Facebook groups, Clubhouse discussions, and different media platforms that unintentionally trap us into a private space where emotional connections are made. We often label these as manipulative and deceitful practices, with people presenting themselves as mentors and spiritual mothers across the country. They exploit emotionalism to engage with your heartaches and promote a variety of pages that operate in deception.

What we have observed is the church mimicking the world by relying on emotionalism. Many churches provoke your emotions to entice you into buying lies, deception, and counterfeit spiritual leaders—whether they are mothers, fathers, mentors, pastors, prophets, or apostles. We find ourselves caught up in schemes and divisions, embracing emotionalism without discernment. As we navigate this realm, it seems that we have accepted emotionalism in the church, and now God is bringing judgment upon it. What we've done is reproduce emotionally driven individuals who possess knowledge of the Word but lack its application. We may know the fruits of the Spirit according to Galatians 5:22-23, but we haven't been taught how to apply this knowledge in our daily lives. Instead, we continue to be guided into emotionalism.

We know that Paul taught us in 1 Corinthians 13 what love looks like, but we haven't been shown how to apply that knowledge to our lives so that God can be glorified effectively. We have learned how to shout, but we haven't been taught how to truly worship. We often find ourselves waiting for the keyboardist to cue up a song, anticipating the moment when the pastor will begin to "tune up," as if everyone is preparing to line up for a race. Yet, no one understands that the assignment of the psalmist is worship. When Saul called for David, the Bible tells us that as David played the harp, the demons fled because true worship invites God to work among us. Scripture says He comes and dwells with us in worship. David played the harp because Saul understood that by inviting the psalmist in with a pure heart for worship, he could build resistance against the enemy, and the enemy would flee.

> We have accepted the shout without the shift or transformation.

Now, people are prepared and waiting to shout without any real manifestation of deliverance. Musicians have been released to simply play the keyboard and stroke the keys rather than to entertain the Kingdom. I firmly believe that just as Jesus instructed us to pray, we should also worship, because the book of Psalms tells us that He inhabits the praise of His people. Our worship should reflect the words of Scripture: "Thy kingdom come, Thy will be done in earth as it is in heaven" (Matthew 6:10 KJV). There should be a worship experience where heaven invades earth and begins to manifest itself, but instead, we settle for the emotionalism of church.

We have settled for the cry without the completion of the work in our hearts. We have accepted the shout without the shift or transformation, choosing to enjoy a good time rather than experiencing true metamorphosis. We settle for feel-good moments, where a Band-Aid solution is presented to the people without real healing.

The Lord has come to judge the very things we have presented as false models or idols in place of the true jewel. He is here to address the foundation of our worship, exposing false presentations and idols, because He desires to do a genuine work that begins with what we confront internally, not just externally. He is coming to deal with issues that haven't been properly taught, as we have been too focused on appearing good on the outside.

God is here to judge the things that have kept us operating in a carnal mindset, preventing us from aligning with His Kingdom. He designed emotions to alert us to how we feel about something so that we can think reasonably about it. Unfortunately, the enemy comes to steal, kill, and destroy. He manipulates our emotions to lead us into irrational reasoning based on lies, stirring up confusion so we process things in a distorted manner and accept those lies. This manipulation often occurs through emotional triggers. It is my assignment to expose these triggers as the frauds that they are. Many of us have become so comfortable with our triggers that they define us. We might say things like, "I don't like that; that's not how I operate." This is a lie from the pits of hell! You have embraced these lies and allowed them to shape your identity simply because they are comfortably seated in your flesh.

The reality is that everyone has emotional triggers, and when they arise, they should prompt you to recognize, "Okay, I'm feeling uncomfortable." It's like a computer: when you open something from the hard drive, the computer begins processing that item. Then, you click on it to view and examine all the information. When you respond to a trigger in a healthy way, you are like a computer user who opens a file to begin processing all the information and addressing it. For the past five chapters, I have emphasized that God gave us emotions, but

He also granted us authority over them. However, the devil comes in and inflates the lies, allowing emotions to take authority over you.

In chapter five, we discussed "Emotional Me" and the concept of the Wonderful Counselor. We examined the passage in Isaiah where he prophesies about the coming Messiah, referring to Him as Mighty God and Everlasting Father. In this passage, Isaiah states that the government will rest upon the Messiah's shoulders. When I looked up the word "shoulders," I found that it refers to the place where we lay our burdens so that Jesus can carry them. A burden is defined as emotional distress that is too difficult to bear (thefreedictionary.com). Thus, Isaiah prophesied that the emotional distress you face would be carried by the Messiah sent by the Lord, so that you don't have to bear it alone.

Throughout life, time, and various experiences, we come to realize that our natural inclination to connect with things can cause them to become emotional triggers in our lives. It's like an emotional alarm clock that alerts us to discomfort. Triggers can manifest as irritations or as things we have suppressed because we didn't want to confront them. The devil often uses spontaneity; someone may say or do something that reactivates an old thought, bringing it back to the surface along with the original feelings. This can lead to inappropriate responses, as the emotions tied to past trauma, hurt, or pain resurface. Consequently, we learn to manage these feelings in our flesh because the church has been too caught up in emotionalism instead of teaching people how to live holy lives.

This chapter will focus on emotional triggers while reviewing scriptures from Genesis, 1 Peter, and James. As we navigate through life, the fruit of the Spirit—self-control—is essential for believers. I remember a conversation I had in 2008 with an older man who said, "If you can't measure it, you can't manage it." Similarly, I say to you: if you can't measure your emotions and thoughts, you won't be able to manage them, nor will you have self-control. You won't be able to rein in your impulses or bring your body into submission to the Holy Spirit. To measure something means you must be able to identify every little thing you deal with. If you can't manage it—meaning you don't examine, challenge, and position yourself healthily to move forward—you will remain in denial and won't change. If you live in denial, you won't grow or mature. If you don't confront those negative thoughts, you'll stay spiritually immature instead of growing into a deeper understanding of the Word.

OPENING PRAYER

I pray, Father, that triggers will no longer cause distress for the person reading this. As we explore this passage, I pray that someone's life will be illuminated, allowing them to look in the mirror and see their true self—not the version the enemy desired them to see. I pray they will confront and examine their genuine selves so they can align with You. Father, I thank You that we are addressing the internal issues, and every external lie is exposed, released, and laid at the feet of Christ. We give You honor, glory, and praise, in Jesus' name. Amen.

Genesis 4:3-6 states, "When it was time for the harvest, Cain presented some of his crops as a gift to the Lord. Abel also brought a gift, the best portions of the firstborn lambs from his flock. The Lord accepted Abel and his gift, but He did not accept Cain and his gift. This made Cain very angry, and he looked dejected. The Lord asked Cain, 'Why are you so angry? Why do you look so dejected? You will be accepted if you do what is right, but if you refuse to do what is right, then watch out! Sin is crouching at the door, eager to control you, but you must subdue it.'" I love this translation. Here, the Lord tells Cain that he must subdue his emotion of anger and take control of it. Verse 16 goes on to say that Cain leaves and murders Abel.

Often, we focus on the gifts presented to God, but God looked beyond the gifts to see the heart posture of the two brothers. It was their internal motivations when giving the offerings that influenced God's acceptance. As the Father examined Cain, He may have thought, "I need to address that anger within him." In this passage, God challenges Cain by deliberately not accepting his offering. In verse 6, He questions Cain about what he is dealing with internally: "Why are you so angry? Why have you let my decision trigger your heart's anger? Why have you internalized my decision incorrectly?" God is challenging Cain because, in verse 7, He states, "You will be accepted if you do what is right, but if you refuse to do what is right, then watch out!"

God is essentially giving Cain an opportunity to process his feelings healthily so he can understand the rationale behind God's decision, rather than viewing it through the lens of his emotional attachment to rejection. The rejection caused Cain to feel dejected, which means he felt sad, disheartened, and ultimately manifested anger. In this passage, we see that rejection triggers Cain's improper anger. Earlier, I mentioned that God gave us emotions, but His will is for us to have authority over them, not the other way around. The Bible states,

"Be angry, but do not sin." This means that while anger is a valid emotion, it shouldn't lead to sinful thoughts or actions.

When married couples discuss divorce, they often express anger rooted in selfishness—feelings that have gone unchallenged. Often, false ideas implanted in both parties' minds cause confusion, stirring up conflict between them. How you manage your emotions and your responses to others truly matters in the Kingdom. This is why, in verse 7, God tells Cain, "If you do what is right, you will be accepted." He gives Cain an opportunity right there and puts his emotions on notice: "I see that anger operating in you. You've harbored this emotion for so long that you've nurtured and fed it. If you don't change, something destructive will happen."

I wish I were in a classroom where I could ask, by a show of hands, how many of you know that there are certain things you babysit and nurture, which, when triggered, lead you to operate from a destructive paradigm. God says, "You will be accepted. I will accept you and your gift if your heart is right and if your thought processes are aligned." Some people minister, go to work, and call themselves Christians, but God doesn't accept any of that because He looks into your heart and sees that it isn't right. You preach, prophesy, and pray. You might be an intercessor, elder, deacon, evangelist, pastor, teacher, or apostle. You play all these different roles, but God examines your heart and says, "I'm not accepting the seeds you sow unto me."

You are doing this out of routine, giving begrudgingly without even realizing it. All of this mess has gone unchallenged in your life, and you've allowed it to mature to a point where it has become triggers. Every time you hear the words "rape" or "molestation," it stirs up feelings within you. When things don't go your way, you're quick to run and isolate yourself. When you can't control a situation, fear rises, leading to panic attacks. You may have outbursts of anger and feel ready to lash out at others.

Cain is experiencing an emotional response to rejection—he feels unaccepted, unapproved, and unaffirmed. Did you know that seeking affirmation and approval is a major component of life? We all desire validation from those we look up to and honor. However, when your heart isn't right, you develop false expectations. If your heart is wrong, even your understanding of affirmation becomes distorted. The person offering affirmation can't win because your processing of it is tainted. You may think things like, "They only did that because they feel sorry for me" or "They only did that because they know me." You struggle to accept genuine honor and affirmation because you haven't moved past the last person who affirmed you with ulterior motives. As a result, you filter the intentions of honorable and honest people through the lens of those who have dishonored you.

Emotional triggers are automatic responses to how others express their feelings, such as anger or sadness. Often, these triggers stem from emotional individuals who haven't learned how to process their feelings effectively. God reassures us that He doesn't hate us or love us any less; He simply cannot accept our gifts when they come from the wrong heart. Sometimes, we can't see the bigger picture because we focus too narrowly on our emotions. God never said He would withdraw His love from us. He tried to prevent Cain from slipping into deeper emotional turmoil that could lead to sin. As our Father, He sought to rescue him and guide him back before he made a grave mistake. He offered Cain the chance to correct his heart, emphasizing that he still had time to make things right. The real issue lies within us, not in what others do.

This passage highlights that the problem is not with God—He is love, and everything He does is rooted in love. The Bible says He chastises those He loves. So, how can we misinterpret a word of correction from the Father when we know Him to be love? The issue is internal; there's nothing wrong with God.

Emotional triggers are automatic and often irrational responses to the emotions of others. In our discussions about emotions, I've mentioned how irrational thinking can arise when we embrace our feelings in unhealthy ways. Trauma plays a significant role here; it is defined as severe emotional or mental distress caused by an experience. This term is crucial in understanding this passage because it indicates the emotional connections, we form in response to moments inflicted by people, places, or things.

I previously mentioned that our negative experiences often shape how we interact with people, places, and things. This is why some individuals avoid church; they've had difficult experiences in places of worship. Similarly, people may struggle to connect with others because the person associated with their trauma was once a source of comfort. For instance, drug addicts often avoid the substances that caused them trauma, as those drugs are linked to painful memories.

Trauma is defined as severe emotional or mental distress caused by specific experiences. The distress from these experiences becomes the trigger for our emotional responses. So, what has been your experience? I encourage you to examine yourself and reflect on what has defined those experiences. What thoughts or beliefs have influenced your perspective to the point that they resurface every time those memories arise?

In Cain's case, his trigger was rejection. Although God accepted Abel's gift, Cain felt his offering wasn't good enough. Many people experience this spirit of competition, where rejection stems from a lack of approval. We often feel rejected when we believe we don't measure up. For instance, when someone says, "You could have done this better," we filter that through our feelings of rejection. In our marriages, when things don't go as we wish, we may feel rejected. This often arises from unrealistic expectations, comparing our partners to others without considering their unique love languages and individual wiring. Such comparisons can create a distorted perception of rejection.

When we lack a healthy model of marriage, this false perception can grow. If we dwell on it and accept the lie, it becomes destructive, leading us to seek an escape from the relationship. We begin to judge our partners based on what they do or fail to do, straying from God's command to love. God never promised that love would be perfect or easy, but He did say that if we truly understand love, the truth will reveal any unhealthy attachments to drama and lies we may have believed. When we receive and apply that truth, our emotional responses can fade away. They can no longer coexist with the truth. As Paul noted, the carnal and spiritual natures are in opposition; they cannot dwell together peacefully.

Jesus said that darkness cannot exist in light. Triggers develop when our emotional responses or attachments to trauma go unchallenged. If you haven't surrounded yourself with people who tell you the truth about how you operate or function, you'll end up embracing lies, and those triggers will persist.

So how do we challenge these emotional responses? One way is to surround yourself with truthful, honest people who have God's heart for you. You need to receive the truth that God provides and rely on it as your measuring stick. Remember, I mentioned that if you can't measure it, you can't manage it. You must evaluate the lies against the Word of God, laying them out side by side. Write a list of lies and their corresponding truths and allow the truth to consume the lies so that they no longer have dominion over you.

Let me reference something from verse seven. It states, "You must do it and be its master." If you want another scriptural reference, the Bible tells us to resist the devil, and he must

> You can judge your life by knowing the truth, and the truth will set you free.

flee. To challenge your emotional response, you need to be in the company of those who embody truth. These are people who love you without judgment and who can provide you with the truth of what God says, enabling you to confront the lies. When the Bible says you must subdue it and be its master, it means to resist the devil so he will flee from you (James 4:7). You need to be honest with yourself. This means measuring yourself realistically so you can manage your life effectively. I believe this process requires both self-reflection and support from others. Sometimes, we lack the willpower until we are confronted by those who genuinely care for us. When they initiate a conversation, we begin the process of measuring and managing our emotional responses.

You can judge your life by knowing the truth, and the truth will set you free. We need to mature to the point where we can take God at His word. In 2 Corinthians 5:17, it says, "In Christ, you are a new creation; old things have passed away; behold, all things have been made new." If God has called you to ministry, don't hesitate to step up and fulfill that calling. You must allow Him the space to transform you and make you new. Eventually, trauma can become a testimony. You can say, "I've overcome that; that is no longer my experience or my life." God has placed so much distance between me and drug addiction that the phrase "Once an addict, always an addict" no longer applies to me. The Word declares that in Christ, I am a new creation; old things have passed away and all things have been made new. The Bible also says, "Whom the Son sets free is free indeed."

No one has to remain victims of trauma, such as rape, divorce, molestation, bullying, manipulation, or drug addiction. They can choose to refuse the identity of a victim. Those experiences were moments in life, but they do not define them. When one truly believes in the truth of being made new, as God told Cain, they gain the power to subdue their thoughts and emotions and become their master. The triggers no longer exist because the truth always cancels out lies.

People do not have to define themselves as bad parents. Mistakes made at one point in life do not dictate their identity; they can change and be made new. Similarly, individuals should not allow others to define them or hold them captive to past experiences, as those perspectives often represent lies.

The struggle with affirmation or approval diminishes when individuals understand that God, as He should have been known by Cain, is truly love. If He offers correction, it remains an expression of love. When set free, there is no need to dwell on the names of those who inflicted pain. For instance, there is no need to label the person who committed an act of molestation as nasty, trifling, or horrible because he likely suffered from trauma himself. Recognizing this truth reveals that there was something he dealt with that led him to act against God's nature and harm others.

God desires for him to be saved, but that is a level of maturity that many are reluctant to discuss. People often want to present themselves well in their lives, through phone conversations, and on social media. However, if one still views the person who committed the crime against them without seeing them as an opportunity for God's salvation, the real problem lies within. The acceptance of false narratives is the issue. The Bible states, "Judge not, lest you be judged." Many may not realize that by continuing to cast judgment and engage in name-calling, they are inviting judgment upon themselves. It is crucial to recognize the importance of truth in this process.

God's love surrounds you. Instead of viewing your spouse as the problem, you will see them as someone God wants you to pray for. You will no longer focus on the rapist, the difficult child, or the pastor who wronged you, because God has presented healthy models of truth to you. Like God did with Cain, I come to you to say, "You will be accepted if you do what is right."

Let's revisit the word "acceptance," which is defined as the acknowledgment that someone or something has been accepted, approved, or favored. Many people seek God's favor, but if your heart has not been right regarding the things or experiences in your life, He has not approved certain things for you.

You may not have seen favor operate in your life or witnessed manifestations of blessings because you identify with your experiences rather than with the God who has healed those experiences and saved you from them. You still associate with the trauma instead of the testimony. You focus on the time and place of pain rather than the victory that makes you a conqueror. You continue to see the person who hurt you and feel pain instead of seeing the Savior. You view the situation through the lens of chains and shackles rather than freedom and liberty. You still identify emotionally with hurtful words. It's astonishing how words can lead one to dark places.

God gives Cain a word of warning, saying, "You will be accepted if you do what is right." He implies that if Cain fixes his heart, he will find acceptance. If he refuses to do what is right, however, he should be cautious; sin is crouching at the door, eager to control him. God grants Cain a moment to reconcile these thoughts, but Cain chooses not to and allows those thoughts to mature.

In James 1:14-15, it states, "But each person is tempted." The New Living Translation adds, "But each person is tempted when they are drawn away by their own desires." What was Cain's desire in this passage? He sought affirmation and approval and feared rejection. He wanted God to show him the same acceptance He showed Abel. However, when Cain was drawn away by his own lust for affirmation, he was enticed because God deemed Abel's gift as superior. What he failed to realize was that it was his heart, not the gift, that mattered.

The Bible says he was disheartened and became sad. This desire for affirmation and acceptance manifested as rejection when it was not given to him. The Bible notes he was dejected or sad, and this emotional trigger was sadness. The experience represented the trauma; the perceived rejection was how he processed that experience. Many people insist on holding onto what they believe is rejection, which often stems from their own lists of grievances. When this desire was conceived, Cain essentially created a storm in his mind, concluding that God had fully rejected him.

He allowed that thought to take root in his heart, nurturing it like a mother with a child. He formed an emotional bond to the trauma, which birthed sin—represented as a baby called sadness—that, in Cain's case, matured into anger. God warned him that when that anger reached its peak, it would ultimately lead to death.

God presented Cain with an opportunity for reconciliation, but Cain's anger had reached a point of no return. He was no longer receptive to God's voice. God was saying, "If you don't reconcile your marriage, you will be cursed. If you don't align yourself with Me, you will remain an addict." Cain's thoughts were complete; he was finished. He no longer wanted to hear the truth of God's word regarding his situation. Instead, he embraced the lies of the enemy, which affirmed his misguided beliefs. This is a common behavior: we often reach out to those who don't trust God the way we claim to, seeking validation for our lies rather than the truth. It's akin to going to a drug house to seek help from someone struggling with addiction themselves. Cain had made up his mind. He felt he didn't need to ponder the truth anymore; he had already decided. James 1:15 illustrates this idea: when sin is fully grown, it leads to death.

You may have already completed your thoughts or shut God out. You might not want to hear what He has to say because you are too caught up in your emotions. You allow your emotions to become your master while turning a deaf ear to God. We shut Him out, ignore His principles, and disregard what He has to say. However, the test isn't over just because you've removed yourself from the situation. You don't advance to the second grade without completing the first. You can't receive a diploma without finishing all twelve grades. You cannot mature in Christ and move to the next level without conquering the test. Yet, many people have turned a deaf ear to God.

In John 5:39, the New Living Translation states, "You search the Scriptures because you think they give you eternal life, but the Scriptures point to Me!" The King James Version says, "Search the Scriptures; for in them ye think ye have eternal life, and they are they which testify of Me." He is saying that even though you may be in the Scriptures and profess your spiritual maturity, you are still not aligned with the simple steps along the way. In your eyes, you think you are on your way to eternity while trying to operate outside of godly principles because you've been triggered by something. He is essentially saying that if you truly knew the Word, your life would testify to it. If you genuinely understood the Word, you would model it—even if you don't fully agree with it. The Word was speaking to Cain in that moment, but Cain responded with, "Nah, I'm good, Lord. I've got this." He chose to fester in his anger and pride, rejecting the opportunity to witness God's glory. He felt too good to let God's love cover a multitude of sins, thinking he had a better way than submitting his life as a living sacrifice, holy and pleasing to God.

Cain was unwilling to let brotherly love continue as a fixed practice, believing he had the right to let love fail. He preferred to detach from the principles of 1 Corinthians 13. Instead of letting go of his emotional triggers and traumas, he chose to babysit those thoughts, allowing them to mature as James 1:14-15 describes. He allowed his anger to manifest into murder. Many of us have been sitting around festering these thoughts, refusing to accept the truths that God has been presenting to us in this hour. He is trying to make us the Church.

The word "murder" is defined as the killing of another person without justification or excuse. We are not justified according to the patterns of the Word when we murder relationships, condemn others, condemn ourselves, or sabotage our own destiny. This situation is twofold: for those who believe they are justified in their wrongdoing; Cain not only murdered his brother but also killed his own destiny. The Bible tells us that God marked Cain and would not allow anyone to kill him; He wanted Cain to experience the consequences of his actions. God emphasized that Cain had no justification or excuse for what he did. If we pay close attention to this passage, we see both homicide and suicide. Cain killed his brother and simultaneously destroyed his own future.

> If your ultimate goal is to gain attention, it's crucial to repent and ask God to help you fix this.

Let's make this relevant to your situation. While we may not have an Abel, we do have our children, spouses, coworkers, nieces, nephews, and grandchildren. As a result, we can end up murdering our relationships with them. Many of us still grapple with anxiety, trauma, pain, hurt, and emotional triggers. We often refuse to accept the truth of what God is saying about our circumstances. Just like Cain, our emotional attachments to situations can lead to spontaneous reactions that harm our relationships with those we care about. Have you ever heard family members say, "I won't be around her because she's too much, always over the top, or acting this way"? That's a form of murder. That relationship has been killed because you're operating from a place of emotion that others find difficult to endure. When you don't confront the issues at hand, you may find yourself using your struggles to seek attention, not realizing that this is a state of immaturity, denial, or even insanity. It is essential to challenge these issues yourself and surround yourself with people who love you enough to help you confront them. If your ultimate goal is to gain attention, it's crucial to repent and ask God to help you fix this.

Another definition for "murder" is something very uncomfortable, difficult, or hazardous. Our thoughts can become hazardous; our emotions can become hazardous. They become difficult to manage when we allow them to take root and manifest. Anger doesn't have to turn into rage. In other words, your emotions don't have to lead to divorce—even within marriage. Emotional distress doesn't have to make you quit your job. Emotional distress doesn't have to isolate you. Instead, you can use your emotions to help you navigate life's challenges.

Many scriptures in the Bible address emotions in various forms, though we don't often teach them that way. Almost every scripture deals with some variation of emotion, because emotions are tied to everything. God himself told Cain that he must do right and master his emotions. The word "subdue" means to subjugate by force, to bring under control by persuasion or other means, to make less intense, or to reduce. This is exactly what many people need to do with certain thoughts they struggle with.

We teach people how to pray, not to control God, but to navigate a realm of spiritual authority through conversation and intimacy with Him. If you're begging God, you aren't breaking yokes. He said, "You shall decree, and it shall be established." So decree and declare that emotional triggers are bound in this hour. We bind every emotional attachment to words, people, places, things, and past experiences, and we place them at the feet of Christ. We bind illegal emotions operating in this house, and we plead the blood of Jesus to flow through our thoughts and minds. As Paul said, we are to have the mind of Christ. I decree and declare that you will have the mind of Christ.

Understand that the mind of Christ represents salvation, victory, overcoming, and conquering. He said you should subdue that thing, and then He said, you should be its master. The word "master" means one who has control over another person, group of people, or thing. In this context, I would add that it's about having control over how a person, place, or thing influences your thinking. You should be the master—no one should be able to trigger you and cause you to lose control.

Take a common example: road rage. We often feel the need to yell at or criticize others when they cut us off. But why must we give others that power? God tells us not to base our emotional responses on how others treat us. Instead, be the master of your response. The enemy will always be on assignment, but that doesn't mean his influence must control us. It means we learn to embrace the fruit of the Spirit called self-control (see Galatians 5:22-23). Let this be part of our prayer: "Lord, continue to grow the spirit of self-control in me. Help me to develop patience and mature in love, so that I can challenge my emotions and thoughts with Your truth."

Let's look at another definition of "master." A master is someone who has control over or ownership of something. God gave you emotions, but they shouldn't own you. You have the power and authority to direct them in whatever way is necessary to maintain godliness. Remember, our role as believers is to process everything through the lens of godly principles.

Another definition of "master" is one who defeats another—a victor. As a songwriter once said, "Victory!" We must always be able to tap into and manifest the fruits of the Spirit. The enemy wants to trap you on a rollercoaster of emotions, but that's not God's plan for you.

You don't have to "kill" or eliminate everything in your life. You don't have to destroy relationships, quit every challenging situation, or push people away just because of how you feel.

Jesus is our example—when He was insulted, He did not retaliate; when He suffered, He did not threaten revenge. Instead, He left His case in the hands of God, who always judges fairly.

We are not called to cast judgment on others but to place our situations in God's hands so He can judge them righteously. How much more glory could be revealed in your life if you surrendered your circumstances to God, letting Him judge according to His Word rather than your emotions?

We need to release the notion of letting our feelings lead us. If our emotions aren't aligned with the Word and go unchallenged, they can lead to deception. Emotional distress can weaken our spiritual reality if we allow it to override godly principles. Then, all we want is escape—from the feelings themselves. If we don't pay attention and challenge these feelings, we can become enticed, lusting after freedom from our emotions rather than seeking God's truth.

This may lead us to think, *If I just move, quit, or get divorced, I'll feel better.* But the reality is, unless our thinking changes, we'll carry the same mindset. You may divorce the person, but not the thought; you may leave the job, but still think the same way. Even if you throw away items from a past relationship, the unresolved thoughts remain inside you. True change comes not from escaping our situations, but from renewing our minds and aligning our thoughts with God's truth.

After pastors cast out all the demons and guide you through deliverance, you still need to walk in your deliverance. Why? Because, although the demon has been cast out, the memory of the situation remains. Just as God told Cain, you must learn to subdue and master those thoughts. When you embrace a healthy, godly mindset, you won't respond destructively to your emotions in every situation. Instead of tearing things down, you'll wait for God to build you up, to judge those things, and to have His way in each situation.

When you've reached maturity, your trials and traumas will transform into testimonies. You won't feel hurt, angry, or distressed every time you recall what happened. For example, one of the major traumas in my life was being molested. Now, I can pray for that person—I don't even remember their name at this point, because God has healed me and freed me from that place. I pray that they, too, find Christ.

We all handle emotions differently, but if they go unchallenged, they can lead us to act destructively. Have you ever considered that the person who caused your trauma might have been dealing with their own unchallenged trauma? Maybe they never sought counsel or placed their pain at the feet of Christ. Perhaps they had no one to confide in, so they managed their thoughts irrationally—the same way many of us do now. Just as Cain acted destructively, they too may have been influenced by untreated wounds.

Perhaps they were molested, struggled with perversion, or dealt with addiction, as modeled by those around them. Have you ever paused to process, in a healthy way, that the reason they inflicted trauma on you might have been because they, too, needed saving? They needed a Savior. This isn't to justify their actions but to acknowledge that they needed help—help they might never have been offered. This is why Scripture says that *love covers a multitude of sins.*

I've counseled many people who have admitted to molesting others or abusing their spouses. I have shown them no less love. They had triggers, difficult situations, and moments of weakness, but I showed them the same love, because God commands it. He alone is the one who judges fairly, as it says in 1 Peter 2:23. We need to reach a place where we don't retaliate, and I bind the spirit of retaliation in Jesus' name. Many of these people have moved on, yet some of us are still holding on to anger, still calling them "trifling" or worse because we're stuck in that moment—not them.

I have also counseled those who were victims of trauma, as well as those who have repented after committing molestation or assault. Some of these individuals have found freedom and healing, and they no longer act in those destructive ways, because they've turned to God. Meanwhile, some victims remain trapped, carrying the pain. So, we bind the spirit of Cain, the spirit of revenge, and we place it at the feet of Christ. For anyone wrestling with thoughts of vengeance, remember the Bible says, "Vengeance is mine, says the Lord." If your thoughts don't model love, you have work to do. It will mean revisiting those painful situations and bringing your thoughts into alignment with God's Word.

Let's talk about those moments when we're triggered. Do you recognize how you feel when that happens? God didn't call you to panic. He calls you to peace. Take a moment to listen to your body—notice the sweaty palms, the racing thoughts. Learn to step back and give yourself a moment to process. Sometimes, we need to pause and acknowledge what we're feeling.

Have you ever stopped to consider the other person, even the one who caused you harm? What do you know about what they've been through? We often get angry at people, but the root of these issues is the enemy. We end up mad at people when the real culprit is the devil. No one is born wanting to hurt others. As life experiences happen these thoughts and behaviors are learned.

These moments remind me of the importance of embracing deeper truths in life. We don't always know if someone has been physically or mentally abused, or how that rejection shaped them—like it did for Cain. So, when we take a step back, we must examine the roots of our own behaviors and beliefs, digging deeper than just seeking closure. This isn't about closure; it's about walking in truth. Closure can sometimes be a lie from the enemy, while truth brings true freedom. The enemy is ultimately at the root of many destructive patterns in people's lives; he comes to kill, steal, and destroy. The wounds he inflicted on others can lead them to impact our lives, too. To walk in liberty, we need to be curious about our struggles and seek the real, deeper answers.

    We must also keep an open mind because God, who judges all things fairly, judges us fairly as well. He doesn't just consider what others did to us; He cares about how we responded. Did we master our emotions? Did we bring our thoughts under control, as He instructed Cain? God gave Cain a way to heal from his emotional distress, and it's the same for us. God sent His Son so we could be free from the deception that overtook Adam and Eve. Unlike them, we have the Holy Spirit living within us, and we're called not to grieve Him with carnal thoughts or behavior. When we respond to others' emotional distress with compassion, rather than escalating the situation, we bring God's peace into it.

    When people mess with our "baby," we may want to lash out and fight, but God is watching to see if we will choose to show love instead. Embracing negative or vengeful thinking allows the enemy to work through us. Galatians 6:1 tells us: "Dear brothers and sisters, if another believer is overcome by sin, you who are godly should gently and humbly help that person back onto the right path. And be careful not to fall into the same temptation yourself." If we're operating in the flesh, are we truly conduits of God's Spirit, or are we conduits of carnality? God gave Cain the chance to come out of his emotional distress and trauma. He gave him an opportunity to challenge his destructive thoughts of murder and revenge, saying, "Subdue those thoughts, become their master, and don't allow them control over your life."

I once asked God to take these struggles from me, and then I did the work. I applied everything Scripture teaches. I let the Holy Spirit deal with me, allowed mentors to guide me, and even sought counsel. Though these moments often felt like correction and chastisement, I stayed, knowing that correction was meant for my growth, not my harm. If you run away whenever someone points out things you don't like about yourself, you'll never be fit for God's kingdom work because you'll always be led by your flesh. You'll flee from those God has placed in your life to help heal you. Correction brings redirection. People need to point out the issues and false beliefs we carry; otherwise, we remain in denial.

When I finally sat in counseling, I was in a dark place. It took me 20 years to confront the trauma of being molested, and I never told anyone in my family. My counselor held a mirror to my face and said, "Look at yourself. Yes, you're hurting from that experience, but it happened 25 years ago. Today, you wake up every day as though it just happened. Now let's address those false thoughts you've allowed to remain in your mind—those perceptions and expectations of healing without growth." The counselor had me look in that mirror and asked, "Do you see the lies? The deception? The self-condemnation? Now let's work to remove them." God wants to heal you and bring you home. He alone has the grace to deal with every broken part of you, just as He did with Cain. God told Cain, "If you do what is right, I will accept you." God calls us to righteousness and offers us a new way of thinking.

The Bible says in John 3:16, "For God so loved the world that He gave His only begotten Son, that whoever believes in Him should not perish but have everlasting life." Jesus didn't come to condemn the world, but so that it would be made whole. God wants you to come home. He invites you to let Him challenge the false beliefs and wounds, so that you no longer carry trauma in unhealthy ways. When you allow Him to reshape your thinking, you'll experience true freedom and healing.

Closing Prayer

Heavenly Father, thank You for what You've released in this moment. Father, I love You, and I thank You for Your deep love for Your people. Even now, I hear You say that You are challenging us to face those harmful thoughts and difficult memories. You're calling us not to suppress them, but to be truly free from them, so they no longer hold power over us. Anything that has the authority to control or shift our emotions has influence over us. Anything that can pull us outside of Your will or cause us to navigate from a mindset against Your truth is something we haven't yet subdued.

Father, I thank You for shining a light on these areas of our hearts so that we can see clearly through the lens of Your truth. Tear down the false perceptions we have about our experiences, so that they no longer act as triggers in our lives. I pray that we would no longer have to ask others to avoid certain topics or shield ourselves from painful memories, because we are truly free from those thoughts and ideals. Lord, may we look at those who have wronged us with hearts full of forgiveness. May we release such powerful forgiveness that instead of cursing, we can truly bless them. Father, I thank You that we are growing to live in alignment with Your word and Your will. In Jesus' name, Amen.

Emotional Me Check-In: How are you Feeling?

Find a quiet space to reflect and invite God into your time of prayer. Use the **Emotional Me Check-In** questionnaire to honestly assess your feelings, their triggers, and any Scripture that speaks to them. Release your emotions to God, seek peace, and consider any actions, like reconciliation or serving others. Reach out for support if needed, and close with gratitude.

1. What am I feeling right now? Can I name this emotion before God?

2. How would I describe this feeling in prayer to God?

3. What does the Bible say about this kind of emotion?

4. How could trusting God impact the way I respond to this emotion?

5. What step can I take to seek peace, healing, or forgiveness in relation to this feeling?

NOTES

Chapter Seven

LOVE: THE ROOT OF HEALTHY EMOTIONS

No one can teach you how to walk in the supernatural, no matter where you're called whether it's ministry, the marketplace, or anywhere else. As leaders, we cannot focus solely on pushing you toward the supernatural if your natural life is dysfunctional. We talk about the fruits of the Spirit and the importance of allowing the Holy Spirit to inhabit you so that your natural self-submits to the Holy Spirit.

We've been on this journey called "Emotional Me." We've discussed the foundation of emotions and the warfare that comes with them. We've talked about wounds and scars and how God is our Wonderful Counselor. We even addressed being honest with yourself so that you can seek counsel from God and trusted voices. If you never overcome your emotions, your life will be chaotic. Failing to address chaotic thoughts and negative emotional connections allows past hurts to keep you stagnant, complacent, and comfortable with being wounded. Without bringing these things under the Holy Spirit's submission, life remains chaotic. Just as we are indoctrinated by the Word of God, all of life involves indoctrination.

Indoctrination is the process of learning principles to live by. Often, we think of it in terms of being grounded in God's Word, but it also applies to everyday life. Each day, we learn something new. When you go to college, you're indoctrinated according to the principles and practices of your chosen field. You acquire the knowledge needed to build a career in that area. When you form new relationships, you're learning how to relate to others. In dating, you're introduced to different principles and life paths to understand each other. When raising children, you adapt your approach to meet each child's unique needs, constantly learning as you go. Even at a new job, orientation serves as a means of indoctrination, teaching you the bylaws, rules, and regulations of that company so that you know how to operate within it.

Everything involves indoctrination. It's the process of learning information about a particular thing—be it a system, person, place, environment, or atmosphere—so you can understand how to navigate it. False doctrine is mentioned in the Bible, referring to when people adopt false beliefs. If you date someone who cheats on you, they have a false doctrine of love. If you encounter someone who's racist, they're indoctrinated by hate. According to TheFreeDictionary.com, to "indoctrinate" means "to instruct in a body of doctrine or principles." Doctrine itself refers to principles or beliefs presented by a group—whether religious, political, scientific, or philosophical—intended to be accepted or believed.

When Satan approaches Adam and Eve at the tree, he's attempting to indoctrinate them with lies. It's all about influencing their acceptance of a belief. How you believe, what you believe, and what you accept as your beliefs are crucial. Indoctrination even happens through trauma: trauma can lead you to believe, for instance, that "all men are untrustworthy" because one man was untrustworthy. You've been indoctrinated by accepting or believing this as a truth. Similarly, a man may believe "all women cheat" because one woman did. We sometimes adopt false principles based on single traumatic events, and they shape our beliefs and behaviors.

Paul tells us, "We don't wrestle against flesh and blood but against rulers, authorities, powers of this dark world, and spiritual forces of evil in the heavenly realms" (Ephesians 6:12, NIV). A principle is an essential quality, law, or moral rule. Some people have distorted morals. Their idea of love might be perversion, which becomes a principle they live by. Perversion creates a belief system—a doctrine—that governs their actions. In the business world, these are known as "operating procedures." These principles form the guidelines for how a company functions, based on foundational beliefs about how to operate. On the other hand, a harmful experience in your life may shape a principle you live by, though it's not rooted in truth or love.

One of the major things the enemy seeks to taint, destroy, disrupt, confuse, and blur is doctrine. The doctrine of love, as stated in 1 John 4:8, says, "Anyone who does not love does not know God, for God is love." The essence of who Satan is, is to corrupt every understanding of love in a believer's life—whether it's love for themselves or love for God—because we draw strength from God. Scripture says, "The joy of the Lord is your strength," and in our weakness, we are made strong in Him. Paul says he would rather boast in his weaknesses so that the power of Christ may rest upon him. So, the very essence of who God is, is the epitome of love. Love is expressed in many ways, through a multitude of principles and doctrines throughout Scripture. God laid that pattern for us throughout the Bible.

Some of you are struggling to give yourself fully to your spouse because you still carry a tainted, distorted perspective of your sexuality. The enemy infiltrated that area of your life when you were young, often through the trauma of rape. As a result, certain things you've done—or won't do—are influenced by the trauma, and you've been indoctrinated by that painful experience. This has made it difficult to be free to express yourself intimately with your spouse. Every time they ask for that, no matter what Scripture says, you are reminded of how the enemy tainted your understanding through that painful experience. You don't have a healthy perspective because you are still looking at things through the lens of the hurt you experienced when you were younger.

The enemy has tainted your view of love, or maybe you didn't have a male figure in your life and were told to just be strong. In doing so, you took on burdens that God designed for a man to carry. You've had to be the strong one when He called you to femininity. You hear the Bible's teaching about how a woman can win her husband with a meek spirit, but for so long you've had to be strong that you approach him like a man. You refer to him in a way that disrespects him, and he does the same to you. The principle—the doctrine—of having a healthy male figure in your life was taken from you, so you were never properly indoctrinated into understanding what a real man or woman looks like.

OPENING PRAYER

Heavenly Father, we come before You with hearts full of gratitude, acknowledging Your love that is the foundation of every healthy emotion. We thank You for the work You've already begun in us and for the healing that is unfolding. Your love is the root of all that is good, and we invite it to permeate every area of our lives, bringing peace, joy, and wholeness. As we walk in Your love, may it transform our hearts, heal our emotions, and help us love ourselves and others as You have loved us. We honor You, we praise You, and we give You all the glory, for Your love is the power that heals and restores. In Jesus' name, Amen.

All of life flows from the single principle called love. If the devil can distort your understanding of love, confuse your ideology about it, or lead you to a flawed view of love, then everything that stems from your love will be conflicted. Paul tells us in 1 Corinthians 13 that if we don't understand love, we are nothing. In essence, your love for yourself and how you view yourself becomes flawed. The love you express and the personality you present are also flawed. Satan's goal is to separate you from God, and he uses traumatic experiences to do so. This is why Paul says, "I will let nothing separate me from the love which is in Christ Jesus." Love is found in God because God is love. The enemy seeks to use these principles to cause separation from God.

If you pay attention, you'll notice that Satan often uses things you can see tangibly to throw you off course from the divine realities that are invisible. We are naturally inclined to focus on tangible things. If you want scripture, look at the story of Saul. He was anointed and promoted to be king of Israel. After witnessing all the supernatural signs and manifestations of God, the people still felt uneasy because they longed for a god they could see. Our natural inclination as believers, when we operate in our carnality, is to desire tangible things. We seek a visible offender because we don't want to consider the possibility that it could be Satan. It's easier to believe that it was someone and not Satan working through them as the influence.

We desire a king, and that king is often defined as someone whose influence has been enlarged. We long for something tangible that can impact us in a big way, even if it is harmful. When bad things happen, our natural inclination is to point the finger at something we can see. We blame others, or our jobs, without realizing that it's the enemy working through a person, place, or thing. Satan will throw a curveball to make you focus on the visible and miss the spiritual influence behind it. Why? Because he knows that his principles will lead you to hate, seek revenge, experience trauma, pain, and anger. You'll take that out on people and forget that it's Satan at work.

The enemy has a strategy: he comes to steal, kill, and destroy. But we forget that he uses people, places, and emotions to carry out his plans. As a spirit being, Satan needs a host to operate in the earth realm, just as the Holy Spirit does. He needs an invitation, and we give him access when we worship our lust, perversion, and anger. In those moments, we invite the enemy in, and he inhabits our thoughts and actions.

Satan understands the power of worship—when you praise or sing, it increases. It increases your capacity to sin and grows stronger when you engage in sinful behavior. But when you worship God, it releases the Kingdom and strengthens your spiritual capacity. Both the enemy and God operate by the same principles. It's never just about the person or the thing; it's about the principle.

We're living in the times described in Revelation. Satan wants to present a law to you that you will live by much like the signs on the road. Those signs represent principles you must abide by. Satan, like a lawmaker, presents his agenda, hoping you'll sign on to it. But our King, Jesus, comes to veto and overturn the enemy's laws and principles.

Let me focus on love. Love is a drive, something deeply ingrained in our psychology. In the realms of science and psychology, a drive is defined as an urgent basic need pressing for satisfaction, often rooted in physiological tension, deficiency, or imbalance—such as hunger or thirst—that compels an organism to act. A drive influences behavior and motivates action. Love, therefore, is a part of your human drive. It's not merely a feeling; it's something you choose to do.

> What you don't realize is that how you love yourself is ultimately how you will love others.

In psychology, love is seen as a strong motivating tendency or instinct related to self-preservation, reproduction, or aggression, prompting activity toward a particular objective. Love is all about choices. It involves embracing a mindset that leads you to act and behave in a certain way here on earth.

The word "drive" is defined as the urge to achieve or reach an objective. Love is a drive—it comes because it has a goal or objective it wants you to achieve. John 3:16 says, "For God so loved the world that He gave His only begotten Son, that whoever believes in Him should not perish but have everlasting life." Then, in verse 17, it says, "For God did not send His Son into the world to condemn the world, but that the world through Him might be saved."

Love, then, has the objective of making you whole. You must choose to operate in love. It's not a mere feeling or emotion. That's why I titled this chapter "Love: The Root of Healthy Emotions." When you learn to love God, you will learn to love yourself. You'll begin to embrace His principles, His doctrine, and rely on them in your life.

When you think about Galatians 5:22-23, which speaks about the fruit of the Spirit, these qualities are rooted in love. They come from the Father, sent from heaven. When He ascended on high, He sent the Holy Spirit to dwell within you, to introduce truths about yourself. That's why, when God starts doing new things in your life, He often begins by challenging how you feel about yourself.

What you don't realize is that how you love yourself is ultimately how you will love others. In scripture, it says, "Love your neighbor as you love yourself." The expectation is that you understand the godly way to love yourself, so that you have a healthy foundation of love and are able to love others well.

When I'm counseling married couples, if I see one spouse treating the other badly, the first thing I say is, "That's how they love themselves." What's in your heart eventually comes out of your mouth. When I see a husband belittle his wife or a wife belittle her husband, the first thing I think is, "What's wrong with them?" Remember, in the last chapter, I said that triggers happen when emotional distress goes unchallenged. Triggers are responses to how we feel that impact others. Someone may do something, but it triggers something else in you, causing you to respond in kind.

He said, "Love your neighbor as you love yourself." So, when I see people who always speak harshly to others, cussing people out or constantly having issues, I say to myself, "That's how they love themselves." That's how they've been conditioned to love. I wonder what happened to them that caused them to express their love this way. I wonder what resides inside of them that has gone unchecked, hidden, and stored away, allowing them to operate in this manner for so long.

Paul helped us define what love is in 1 Corinthians 13. He said love is patient and kind. It does not envy or boast, it is not arrogant or rude. It does not insist on its own way. In essence, it is not selfish. When I see selfish people operating selfishly, only thinking about themselves, I always go back to the fact that they don't understand love. Love is not irritable. If you get irritated by every little thing, every ism and schism about people that defines them or makes them who they are, and it irritates you, you don't understand that people should be able to be themselves around you without causing irritation.

> **When we are conduits and models of love, our behavior expresses love.**

He says love is not resentful. It does not rejoice at wrongdoing. We don't intentionally do wrong things. We don't operate outside of our covenants and commitments on purpose. He says love rejoices with the truth. We don't run from the truth. If you run away from the truth,

140

and no one can ever tell you anything or constructively criticize you, you need to get it together. If you always need a cheerleader, someone to put a Band-Aid on you, pat you on the back, and you can't handle the truth about yourself, you don't understand love.

He says love bears all things. If you are a quitter, if you run away from things, if you can't stand firm in your commitments, on God's word, godly principles, or your assignments, then you don't understand love. If you struggle with faith, if you doubt God's words because they're not coming to pass on your timeline, if you can't believe that the joy of the Lord is your strength, then you don't understand love. If you can't believe Philippians 1:6, "Being confident of this very thing, that He who began a good work in you will complete it until the day of Jesus Christ," you don't understand love.

He says love endures all things. This means you've learned how to endure and still maintain godly composure. You don't walk away mumbling when things don't go your way. He says love never ends. In essence, this is a choice we make daily because love is a drive that the Kingdom operates on. God is love, and because God lives in us, we are made in His image, but we are born into sin. Our only conduit for love, when we choose it, is when we act in love. When we are conduits and models of love, our behavior expresses love.

We choose love daily. When a car cuts us off, we choose not to cuss someone out. We choose love when we want to quit—whether it's our family, marriage, or job—but we stay the course. We choose love when we're wronged by our loved ones, but we continue to love.

Hebrews says, "Let brotherly love continue," and let it be a fixed practice; never let it fail. We must never let love lose. When we learn to love ourselves, our self-love should never end. It shouldn't be tainted or derailed by traumatic experiences. Our self-love has to be so secure that we embrace biblical principles concerning self-control.

When our emotions threaten to take us on a roller coaster, we resist. If we receive the notion that we should respond in anger, we resist Satan, and he must go. Love never ends; we should never stop loving ourselves.

That's why the scripture says, "In Christ, you are a new creation. The old has passed away; behold, the new has come." We've been indoctrinated by our past, but now we can embrace the new love that God has given us. We are created in His image and called to be Christ-like. Now we can love ourselves.

Love is the root of healthy emotions. Paul says, "As for prophecies, they will pass away; as for tongues, they will cease; as for knowledge, it will pass away but love never ends." 1 Corinthians 16:14 says, "Let all that you do be done in love." We must be indoctrinated to be habitual lovers of ourselves, of God, and of others. Why? Because if we learn to embrace godly principles, our emotions will form healthy models of expression and become healthier.

We use 1 Corinthians 13 as a model to judge our own behaviors. Why? Because love is a drive—it is a principle that can direct our behavior. It's not a feeling. If you say, "I'm falling out of love," you've simply decided to stop loving. You've chosen to no longer love your spouse, others, or even things. If your doctrinal perspectives on God and life aren't in agreement, you can't walk together. You can't force them together. They'll never glue and form a union, even if you put a ring on it. Love is a choice, and we are mandated to love.

1 John 4:15-21 says, "Whoever confesses that Jesus is the Son of God, God dwells in him, and he in God. And we have known and believed the love that God has for us. God is love, and he who abides in love abides in God, and God in him."

When you're operating outside the realm of love, your expression of love is operating outside the will of God, because God is love. He says that if you operate in love, then you are in God. If your behavior aligns with the pattern described in 1 Corinthians 13, then you are operating in God, and God is in you.

> The fear of things not changing causes you to walk outside of God's love.

Verse 17 says, "Herein is our love made perfect, that we may have boldness in the day of judgment; because as He is, so are we in this world." He's saying that we are made perfect in our love because it brings boldness to us on the day of judgment. When we operate in love, it gives us the courage to stand against anything in this world that seeks to judge or come against godly systems.

When you operate in love, your love is perfected. This boldness allows you to stand firm, just as Christ did, in the face of opposition. When things try to pull you away from 1 Corinthians 13, the love of God inside you will prevent those things from affecting you or your emotions. You have the boldness to stand firm in the face of the world's pressures, just as Christ did.

Verse 18 says, "There is no fear in love." This is one of my and my wife's favorite scriptures. If you are standing here as Christ was in the world, remember that if fear strikes you, it is not from God. In this passage, we see how God and love are parallel: God is love. There is no fear in love because perfect love (or God) casts out fear. When God is in you, He casts out fear.

Hebrews 11:1 says, "Faith is the substance of things hoped for, the evidence of things not seen." Without faith, it is impossible to please God. When you move away from God's love and faith, you enter into Satan's realm, where he ministers fear to you, while God ministers faith. If you allow yourself to be indoctrinated by fear, you accept it as truth. A doctrine is something presented and accepted as truth, so when you accept fear, it begins to torment you.

How does fear torment you? It affects your emotions. Every time you fear, it sparks an emotional reaction, launching you into an emotional war. You become an emotional rollercoaster because you've left God's love and chosen fear. You've exchanged emotional stability (the love of God) for emotional instability (Satan's fear). Fear torments you because you can't rest at night when your mind is racing with thoughts of failure or fear that the promises of God will not come to pass.

The fear of things not changing causes you to walk outside of God's love. Love, as defined in the Bible, includes a concern for God, for His principles, and for others. Ultimately, concern for God is synonymous with concern for yourself, because God is concerned about you. He gave His Son for you. These are expressions of love that God wants you to learn and embrace. He wants you to love Him, to live by His principles, and to love others and yourself.

When you learn to love God and His principles, everything about you changes. Romans 12:2 says, "Do not be conformed to this world, but be transformed by the renewing of your mind." This transformation is necessary so you can prove what is the perfect will of God. By understanding and embracing God's love and principles, you can maintain a healthy mind. Without belief in God's love, fear will torment you, causing you to toss and turn all night, always on guard, never trusting others.

Be careful, however, when God asks you to trust others. He has already told you He is your provider and protector. He wants you to live boldly. As 1 John 4:17 says, "Herein is our love made perfect, that we may have boldness." When our love is perfected, we can stand boldly against paranoia, depression, sadness, rage, rejection, and the need for approval. We can stand boldly because we are approved and affirmed by God.

Verse 19 says, "We love Him because He first loved us." This is the foundation of everything we've discussed. John is saying that he loves God simply because God first loved him.

Do we love God enough to trust that He loves us? Do you have the assurance in your heart and mind that God truly loves you? If so, then abide by His principles. That's what John is saying. Remember the definition of love I just gave you. He says, "We love Him because He first loved us." This means we are concerned about God and His principles because He has already been concerned about us. He made promises to us, knowing us before we were formed in the womb. He told us we are fearfully and wonderfully made. He called us according to His purpose. He didn't come into this world to condemn us, but that we might be made whole. His love is tied to our holistic health.

John goes on to say, "If a man says, 'I love God,' and hates his brother, he is a liar." You can insert anything you want in that space where "brother" is. If you say you love God, but hate others, you are lying.

If a man says he loves God but hates his wife, or if a woman says she loves God but hates her husband, or if anyone says they love God but harbor hatred toward anything else, they are a liar. Why? Because all love is given to us by God. If a man claims to love God but hates his job, he is a liar. Why? Because God is the God of provision; He is Jehovah Jireh, my provider. You can fill in the blank with anything you want because it is all mandated by God.

1 John 4:20 says, "For he who does not love his brother whom he has seen, how can he love God whom he has not seen?" So, what is your blank? What do you need to call out? A significant part of this passage is about being concerned that others see your true self because

you struggle to love yourself. Verse 17 states, "When you walk fully in love, you can be bold." So again, what is your blank? You may need to come out of that place of bondage so you can be set free from your blank.

You might be like a trauma hoarder, holding onto your past hurts, which is why you can't find freedom. Verse 17 reminds us that when our love is made perfect, we can walk in boldness. So, what is your blank? Stop hoarding your trauma. It's like having a room full of junk that you haven't been real enough to let go of. You need to release it to God and share it with trusted voices.

If you truly love God, you will love yourself, your brothers, your sisters, and His provision. You might just need a "pessimism detox." You might not even realize that pessimism is an expression we embrace when we don't understand that God cares for all of it. He loved us through our struggles, and His Son died for them. Love is the root of healthy emotions. When you allow the doctrine of love to manifest in your life, it becomes easy to love yourself, love others, and trust God at His word.

The definition of pessimism is a tendency to stress the negative or unfavorable and to take the gloomiest possible view. So, if you are always looking through the lens of fear, you are never happy or excited about anything. This mindset is how you have been indoctrinated. When hell rules your life, you view everything through a negative lens, seeing nothing positive.

Hope and faith represent optimism, the opposite of pessimism. You learn to look at life through a positive lens, desiring and hoping for favorable outcomes. You don't let anything bring you down; you don't retreat into a cave because you know how to encourage yourself. The Bible says that David encouraged himself in the Lord. When you love yourself, you learn to encourage yourself, and you should embrace a lifestyle of worship in song and prayer.

If you're struggling to break through in worship or find it hard to manifest in prayer, in this season, God wants you to focus on prayer. He needs you to make your petitions known so He can act on your behalf. God manifests Himself in prayer because it is an intense form of worship. When you pray, He responds and speaks.

Love is the root to healthy emotions, embracing God's principles, and loving yourself. I invite you to repeat after me:

"Father, I repent for not loving You, myself, or others enough. Father, today I dedicate my life to You. I align myself with the doctrine of love. Father, I pray that 1 Corinthians 13 becomes a model I habitually apply in my life and living. Father, take away everything that has tainted my understanding of love and fill those spaces in my heart and mind with Your love. In Jesus' name, I pray, Amen."

When love is your behavioral expression, you are compelled to love yourself, love God, and love others. Love binds us all together in perfect harmony. Harmony is defined as a relationship in which various components exist together without destroying one another. Therefore, when you choose to love, it becomes your legal obligation to operate in harmony. When we operate in love, we will not destroy each other, because love is our obligation, not an option. You understand that because God is love. He can bring about a metamorphosis in your marriage, relationships, job, or whatever that may be. You are legally obligated to stand firm in that truth.

CLOSING PRAYER

Heavenly Father, I thank You for loving each one of us. I thank You that You are doing a new thing, and that we will perceive it. I thank You that our eyes have been opened and that people will choose to love more deeply. I thank You that they will learn to love themselves, and even when the enemy presents tormenting thoughts, they will embrace Your love as described in John 14:4-17.

May that love be made perfect within them, meaning that love will be complete in You. They will know Your love and stand firm in it, becoming bold against anything that tries to rise up against them, tearing apart their families and self-worth. This transformation will be fulfilled in them, never to return to doubt, fear, or torment.

Father, I thank You for releasing them from all tormenting spirits associated with traumatic experiences. I ask that You redefine love for those who have struggled to express it to their spouses. I thank You that You are freeing them, and that romance will flourish in their lives.

For those who are waiting and dealing with these issues now or in the past, I thank You that when You bring resolution and send that man or woman, they will walk in a realm of liberty. They will experience new love according to Your Kingdom—undefiled, righteous, and filled with favor. Father, I thank You that they will embrace the doctrine of love and walk in it boldly. In Jesus' name, Amen.

Emotional Me Check-In: How are you Feeling?

Find a quiet space to reflect and invite God into your time of prayer. Use the **Emotional Me Check-In** questionnaire to honestly assess your feelings, their triggers, and any Scripture that speaks to them. Release your emotions to God, seek peace, and consider any actions, like reconciliation or serving others. Reach out for support if needed, and close with gratitude.

1. What am I feeling right now? Can I name this emotion before God?

2. How would I describe this feeling in prayer to God?

3. What does the Bible say about this kind of emotion?

4. How could trusting God impact the way I respond to this emotion?

5. What step can I take to seek peace, healing, or forgiveness in relation to this feeling?

NOTES

Chapter Eight

SUPPRESSION, CAVES, SELF-MEDICATION & SILENCE

During this journey called *Emotional Me*, we've seen God do so much, and I'm so grateful that He would do the thing that He does so well, heal and restore. We've taken this journey for seven chapters now; you should give yourself a pat on the back. We talked about different variations of emotions and how God gave us emotions. Emotions were designed to bring awareness to the things that are going on in our lives. They serve as our emotional alarm system, alert system, or notification system. Just like notifications on your phone, when your emotions are operating in a healthy way, they inform you about how you feel about a situation. When your emotions are functioning properly, you can make sound decisions regarding your relationships with people, places, or things.

In the last chapter, we discussed love as the root of healthy emotions. The Lord prompted me to return to that topic because often it's a struggle to reach a place of healthy emotions. We also have to address our responses to emotional distress. In this chapter, we will talk about suppression, caves, self-medication, and silence. These are unhealthy realms that the enemy can push us into when he gains a foothold, leading us into trauma or adverse experiences that can cause our systems to malfunction. This can result in operating outside of the will of God.

These unhealthy responses occur when we don't fully understand the truth about who God is. Remember, emotional triggers happen when our emotions go unchallenged in a healthy way and without the guiding light of truth. We form emotional triggers when our emotional distress remains unaddressed. As these triggers take their toll, we build mechanisms to protect ourselves in various situations. We start to suppress our feelings, retreat into the cave, self-medicate, or remain silent because we feel overwhelmed.

As we go through this chapter, I pray that you will take this journey with me because God never designed us to operate from such a realm; it is an unhealthy space to inhabit. We have convinced ourselves, even though it is not true, that we must suppress our feelings, retreat to the cave, self-medicate, and remain silent.

When we feel like we can't talk about our truth or communicate our situation, that is when the enemy is fully at work. When you turn away from the truth and embrace false perceptions, it causes you to shut down. Let's look at Psalm 32:5 and reflect on the notions of suppression, caves, self-medication, and silence. These are all responses that occur when we fail to operate in truth or lack the guidance of those who can lead us to truth, or when we are simply rebellious or in denial about the truth.

Opening Prayer

Father, we come before You as we address the realm of emotional health, particularly the struggles of suppression, retreating into caves, self-medication, and silence. Lord, we ask that You release wisdom and healing to those who are facing these challenges. We pray that You would open hearts to Your truth, guiding them toward freedom and wholeness. Take control of every thought and word, Lord, and let Your will be done in every area of our lives. May Your peace and understanding reign, and may Your strength empower us to overcome unhealthy patterns. In Jesus' name, Amen.

Psalm 32:5 says, "Finally, I confessed all my sins to You and stopped trying to hide my guilt. I said to myself, 'I will confess my rebellion to the Lord,' and You forgave me. All my guilt is gone. Thank You, Holy Ghost."

David is writing a song to the Lord, reflecting on the various sins he has committed. He has the heart of a worshiper and is confessing his sins to the Lord. He stopped trying to hide his guilt and made the decision to confess everything to God, including his rebellion. We must understand that through this song, David is telling us that when he confessed his rebellion to the Lord, God forgave him, and all his guilt was removed. This is important to know because, many times, when we go through difficult situations, we experience guilt, self-pity, and remorse. These emotions can cause us to shut down, and in trying to separate from the natural things of life, we often end up shutting God out as well. We don't give God the space and room in our lives to rule, reign, and heal us.

Guilt is defined as the responsibility for the commission of an offense, moral culpability, or the violation of a criminal law. We begin to own our mistakes, and while we are responsible for things we've done, we sometimes take on guilt for things that were done to us, which were beyond our control. This unhealthy sense of guilt can lead to shame, creating an emotional wall that isolates us. Another definition of guilt is the painful emotion experienced when one believes their actions or thoughts have violated a moral or personal standard. It's an emotional experience that arises when someone has wronged us. This internalized pain, combined with the pain inflicted by others, forms a realm of guilt. If not confronted and checked, guilt can become an unhealthy emotional trigger. Once these walls are built, it becomes difficult to handle them because we're operating from an unhealthy perspective.

David says, "I confess my rebellion to the Lord." He acknowledges that he was operating outside of God's will, but God forgave him. As guilt manifests and grows, we may find ourselves operating in rebellion, avoiding the truth, and refusing to let others speak truth to us. We may go into denial, aggression, anger, depression, anxiety, or stress, continuing in a state of rebellion and disobedience. If left unchecked, we suppress our emotions, retreat into silence, or try to self-medicate. David speaks from experience, as he himself was the offender who got caught. We all know the story of David and Bathsheba—how he had her husband killed to cover up his adultery and avoid the consequences of his actions. One sin led to another, and it wasn't until the prophet Nathan confronted him that he came to repentance.

It's only when someone challenges us with truth—whether it's God or another person—that these hidden, unhealthy patterns in our lives are exposed. This is why John 8:32 says, "And you will know the truth, and the truth will set you free." This is not just a scripture to quote, but a paradigm, a theological truth that we need to apply to our lives every day. We can't stay trapped in guilt and denial when we know the truth. When emotions are out of control, we must push through the lies to reach the truth. When David was finally able to break through his guilt and shame, he could confess his sins to the Lord.

There is something powerful and healing about confessing your truth to God and to someone who loves you, can remain neutral, and simply listen. David's confession, "You forgave me," means that God assured him, "It's going to be alright. I've washed away your sins." When we understand and know that God has forgiven us, there's a release. We can walk in the freedom of knowing that all our guilt is gone. There's a lifting of the burden when we operate in truth.

But the question is: Do you really believe that God has forgiven you? Have you ever taken your rebellion to the Lord? Not in a superficial way, but honestly bringing your emotions—your hurt, your hatred, your guilt—to God. You may feel angry and not want to forgive, but confessing your emotions to God and asking Him for help is a critical step in healing. Many don't realize that this is an important aspect of sin. David recognized that hiding his guilt was itself a sin. He confessed all his sins to the Lord and stopped trying to hide his guilt. In essence, he was admitting, "I allowed this guilt to fester, and it separated me from You. Lord, I repent for allowing these thoughts and emotions to manifest and hinder my relationship with You."

Have you ever repented for how you handled a situation, blew it out of proportion, or became overly dramatic? Have you walked around feeling disconnected from God, unable to engage fully in church or ministry because you're carrying this emotional weight? David's confession shows that when we carry guilt and shame, it separates us from God's presence. He had to confess his sins, stop hiding his guilt, and let God cleanse him.

David is also speaking as the offender in this story. We need to recognize that those who have wronged us are also carrying their own guilt. Have you ever considered what might have happened in their lives to make them act in that way? David carried guilt for his sin against Bathsheba and her husband. But Bathsheba, too, had to reconcile her own feelings and truth. She allowed the king to have her, to get her pregnant, and ultimately had her husband killed. Yet, despite all the pain, they found redemption in repentance. They had Solomon, one of the wisest men in the Bible. Both David and Bathsheba had to confront their guilt and find forgiveness, and so can we.

God calls us to bring all our burdens to Him. We need to be honest like David and Bathsheba, confessing our sins and seeking God's forgiveness. We must come to God with the truth of how we feel and what we've done, knowing that He will forgive and heal us.

David's experience teaches us that suppression—whether of guilt, shame, or past trauma—only causes more harm. We may try to avoid confronting uncomfortable truths, but God wants us to face them. Jesus came to bring truth and healing, to restore what was broken. In John 14:6, Jesus says, "I am the way, the truth, and the life. No one comes to the Father except through Me." We can't move forward in our relationship with God until we accept His truth.

> Suppressing painful memories or desires distorts our thinking and creates unhealthy patterns.

The practical application of walking in truth is to be real with ourselves and with God. For example, if something happened years ago and we've been suppressing it, we don't have to keep living in that pain. We can let go of those suppressed emotions and allow God to heal us. Suppression is the conscious exclusion of unacceptable thoughts or memories. David said he stopped hiding his guilt because he knew it was only hindering his relationship with God. Suppressing painful memories or desires distorts our thinking and creates unhealthy patterns. Only by confronting these suppressed emotions with God's truth can we experience true healing and freedom.

As Romans 1:18-20 says, "God's anger is revealed from heaven against all the godlessness and wickedness of people who suppress the truth by their wickedness." When we allow sin, trauma, or past experiences to suppress God's truth, we grieve the Holy Spirit. But God wants us to confront those painful truths and allow His healing to restore us.

David's repentance was not just for the offense but for the emotional suppression that led him to rebellion. He realized that the only way to find freedom was through truth. We need to embrace this truth in our own lives—confess, repent, and allow God's grace to heal us. When we stop suppressing our emotions and confronting the truth, we can walk in the freedom and healing that God offers.

Just because someone encounters relationships with men who operate within a certain negative paradigm, it doesn't mean that one bad experience defines all men. We tend to generalize and believe that all men or women are "dogs" because of one painful experience. However, this perception is shaped by the trauma we've endured. You've been hurt, and while you've been healed from it, you never fully learned the wisdom from your past relationship. So, when the next opportunity comes, you find yourself choosing someone who resembles your past partner, and you get hurt again. This cycle continues, and you keep picking partners who remind you of your previous relationships. The next person could be the right one for you, but because you haven't fully healed, they end up bearing the weight of your unresolved pain.

Romans 1:18 says, "But God shows his anger from heaven against all sinful, wicked people who suppress the truth by their wickedness." God is angry when we suppress His truth, choosing instead to cling to the emotional turmoil, trauma, and lies we've experienced. Verse 19 continues, "They know the truth about God because he has made it obvious to them." His eternal power and divine nature are evident to us, so there is no excuse for denying Him. God's anger arises when we refuse to embrace truth, instead suppressing it with our painful experiences. He says, "I have given you ample evidence of My existence: every day you wake up to My creation, yet you still deny the truth of who I am."

You wake up each day with breath in your lungs, when I could have called you home. You see My hand at work in your finances, health, and provision, yet you still deny Me. Just like David, you've seen the lions and the bears, but you still refuse to let Me bring healing and truth into your life. The wickedness of what happened to you has taken hold of you, and you continue to suppress the truth that I sent My Son so you could be free. You keep managing the pain instead of seeking true freedom from it. The truth, when embraced, will set you free. But you must choose to allow that truth to come into your life.

Some of you have been denying the truth for so long that it's hard to recognize it when it's right in front of you. This is what Romans 1:18 is addressing: the evidence of God's truth is evident, yet we fail to embrace it. God is angry because you profess to know Him, yet you don't fully accept His truth. You can prophesy, pray with power, and lay hands on the sick, and they recover. But, as Scripture says, God might still say, "Depart from Me, for I never knew you." You must come to a place where you surrender completely to God, allowing Him access to every part of your life. You can only serve one master: either God or your trauma. When you suppress your pain, you give power to the very forces that are keeping you bound.

When you yield to these negative forces, their goal is to steal, kill, and destroy your relationship with God. They want to sever that connection because they know if you have a healthy relationship with God, He will expose the enemy's work in your life. The enemy's assignment is to move you into isolation, keeping you silent, self-medicating, and retreating from the truth. He knows that in isolation, he can torment you, keeping you from crying out for help, whether to God or to others who can help pull you out of that darkness.

1 John 4:18 says, "There is no fear in love. But perfect love drives out fear, because fear has to do with punishment. The one who fears is not made perfect in love." The enemy seeks to bring you into fear, but God's love casts out that fear.

Matthew 27:3-5 recounts Judas's remorse after betraying Jesus: "When Judas, who had betrayed him, saw that Jesus was condemned, he was filled with remorse. So, he took the thirty silver coins back to the chief priests and elders and said, 'I have sinned, for I have betrayed innocent blood.' 'What is that to us?' they replied. 'That's your responsibility.' So, Judas threw the money into the temple and left. Then he went away and hanged himself." When you can't escape the tormenting thoughts and the enemy's influence on your emotions, you start destroying everything around you. You kill relationships, joy, love, and everything good that God is trying to bring into your life. Judas, an apostle of Jesus, was surrounded by all the glory of Christ, yet he betrayed Him. He had free will, and had he chosen God, he could have overcome the battle. But he didn't.

This shows how, when emotions are suppressed, they can lead to destructive consequences. Lust, when conceived, brings forth sin, and when sin is full-grown, it brings death. For Judas, the lust for money led to his betrayal, regret, and ultimately, suicide. The enemy desires to lead you to spiritual suicide, convincing you that isolation and retreat are the answers. Some of you are so comfortable in your self-imposed isolation, not realizing that the enemy has already claimed that space. He doesn't need an invitation; you've already welcomed him in. In that silence, he works to keep you trapped, hoping that every opportunity for repentance will be stifled.

> **When suppression matures, fear, isolation, and regret follow.**

Judas's remorse is a powerful lesson: when you've lost peace and given in to the enemy's lies, nothing else matters. The money, the success, none of it matters when your mind is tormented. I've come to realize that peace is essential for me. If you disturb my peace, you can be sure I'll let you know. Peace that surpasses all understanding is non-negotiable, and I will fight for it.

The enemy's strategy is to rob you of peace, pushing you into a realm of suppression. When you're alone and your mind spirals, you've surrendered to confusion. That's why you must cling to truth. God promised that His Word would never return void; it will accomplish what He sent it to do. Similarly, the enemy's confusion works to destroy your peace, like a whirlwind tearing through your life.

Judas felt deep remorse, a painful regret for his actions. This deep regret, a hallmark of both the victim and the offender, is a powerful reminder of the danger of allowing our natural emotions to control us. The story of Judas is a warning to every believer: if we allow our feelings to reign unchecked, we'll end up separated from God. Satan's goal is to suppress your feelings, because when they encounter God, they are healed.

When suppression matures, fear, isolation, and regret follow. Consider 1 Kings 19:8-9, where Elijah, in fear of Jezebel after defeating the prophets of Baal, runs into a cave. God asks him, "What are you doing here, Elijah?" The cave symbolizes a place of fear and separation from God, where peace is lost, and fear reigns. Elijah, in his emotional distress, forgets the power of God and retreats into a place of spiritual desolation. God calls him out of the cave, urging him to step back into the truth.

We often separate ourselves and retreat into a place that's dry, void of the Holy Spirit, and distant from God. If you read the rest of the passage, God tells Elijah to come out of the cave so that he can see His work again. God wasn't in the cave because Elijah ran there out of fear. There's nothing in the cave but mixed emotions, fear, trauma, and confusion. Death and disobedience are signs of a place where God doesn't reside. When we seek seclusion, we shut God out and reject anyone who might lead us back to Him. The last place you want to be is alone in a cave where God isn't.

You must be with God. That's why the scripture says in 2 Corinthians 3:17, "Where the Spirit of the Lord is, there is liberty." You need to get with the Holy Spirit and surround yourself with people who are filled with the Spirit. Stop isolating yourself, especially when you're struggling. That's confusion and denial at work. Get up, seek out intercessors, prophets, and deliverance ministers who know how to pray and discern what you need for freedom. Whatever you do, get out of the cave and go see God.

Situations in life often lead us to become captive, and we let the enemy guide us into the cave, isolating us. We feel weak and confused, and our emotions lead us deeper into that place of isolation. God told Elijah to come out because he needed to see Him again. The cave is desolate—it's a place where your fear, selfishness, and pride fester. You'd rather be in that place than with God. But God says, "Come out, where life is. There's living water here."

God wants to draw you out of fear, trauma, and unhealthy mindsets and back into a relationship with Him. Jezebel threatened you, but God wants you to step out of the cave, and experience breakthrough and healing. Your deliverance is now, and you don't need to stay in that dry, desolate place. You can come out of the cave and be reconciled with God. The cave is the worst place to be—God never called a Christian to run into it. Elijah chose to run into the cave because he couldn't handle life outside of it, but God was calling him to trust in Him.

The cave is not a place for cutting people off; we are meant to build relationships and fellowship with others. When you stop going to church or connecting with people, it's a sign that you've been isolating yourself. It's time to come out of the cave!

Stop suppressing your emotions and self-medicating with substances to cope with depression, pain, or intense feelings. Often, when we can't handle the cave, we try to numb the pain with drugs, alcohol, sex, shopping, or overeating. But we forget that true healing and life are in Christ Jesus.

David had to confess his rebellion to the Lord, and God forgave him, removing all his guilt. Everything you're dealing with can be healed when you live by truth. God never designed us to hide in a closet with alcohol and replay our trauma. We're called to face our giants like David, armed with faith in God, and trust that He will help us overcome. When we walk in truth, God raises up a supernatural standard that leads us to victory. Don't you want to be victorious?

1 Thessalonians 5:8 says, "But let us, who live in the light, be clearheaded, protected by the armor of faith and love, and wearing as our helmet the confidence of our salvation." In essence, we are to be sober-minded, protected by God's faith, love, and the helmet of salvation. We must have confidence in the One who saves us. Do you love God enough to believe that when you bring your struggles to Him, He will save you? Why do we call Him a Savior if we don't believe He can save us? Men, women, drugs, sex, shopping—none of these will save you. They may offer momentary satisfaction, but you'll end up back in depression, confusion, and sin. Why settle for temporary pleasure? God wants you free. He came to make you whole.

Consider all the scriptures in the Bible that remind us God has our back. Why do we forget that when our emotions take control? God wants to set you free—that is His assignment in your life: freedom and liberty from everything you've been through and everything you'll face. God didn't call us to self-medicate or to retreat into denial. Suppression will drive us into the cave, where we think we're hiding our pain, but others see it in the way we withdraw. People already know when you're struggling because they don't hear from you or see you.

You may think you're strong because you're going into your prayer closet, or into your "cave," but those around you are worried because they can see the unhealthy patterns you're developing. While you're isolating yourself, people are calling and texting, trying to reach out, but you're not responding. When you finally say you're okay, everyone knows you aren't. Now, they've moved from faith to worry because you haven't aligned with truth and faith. It creates a domino effect. You operate in an unhealthy way, and those around you begin to do the same. Soon, everyone is walking in fear instead of faith.

The last thing is silence. I love the definition: it's the refusal or failure to speak out, a state of being quiet, of putting doubt and fear to rest. That's what silence, stubbornness, and self-medicating are—willful acts that separate us from the Kingdom. You choose to be silent and cut yourself off from people while turning to substances or unhealthy behaviors. This is what rebellion looks like. Psalm 32:5 shows us that David confessed his sins and stopped hiding his guilt. He said, "I will confess my rebellion to the Lord." Silence, self-medicating, and retreating into the cave are all acts of rebellion against God's command for us to operate in truth.

You've been through abuse, and now you define yourself by that moment. Your emotional distress is tied to that moment. But must everything in your life be defined by that moment? You've made poor decisions, gone through seasons of hardship, and felt poverty, but does that define you? You've been through things, but you don't have to be defined by them, nor do they have to hold you captive.

I shared with you before that I was molested when I was five years old, and that trauma held me until I was 30 years old. From the age of 5 to 30, I struggled with unhealthy emotions, but everything changed when I encountered the truth. God sent someone into my life, a Christian psychologist and I was able to sit with him and get free. I remember telling him, "If all you can give me is science, I don't want it." He told me he was a Christian, and I said, "If you can take what you've learned and show me how it aligns with scripture, I'll show up every week." I knew that only God's truth could set me free. This man had the grace to merge both, and through that, I was set free.

I no longer define myself by what I went through, by my poor decisions, or by my past experiences. People often ask me, as a leader in the body of Christ, how I stand so boldly. I tell them, "You see my 'hood resume,' and that's how you connect with me. But I don't identify with myself through what I did or who I was. I identify with myself through how God sees me." I've been made new. Now, I see myself in the newness of who God says I am. Even in the future, when challenges come, I don't have to define myself by them. I can process through them with emotional health and move forward.

> You can't hold on to the hurt and expect to be set free.

When you learn to process your emotions healthily, you can move on. You don't have to respond to every offense. Jesus taught us in Matthew 5:39 that if someone offends us, we should turn the other cheek—not literally, but to let it go. Let it go in tears, or even through the pain. The point is to release it. You can't hold onto the hurt; you can't hoard your hurt. You have to say, "Lord, that hurt, but You died for that. I don't have to stay hurt. I might have been the victim, but I don't have to stay victimized." Take that truth into your spirit: You might have been the victim, but you don't have to live as one. God wants you free.

God is a deliverer, and He wants to set you free, but you have to be willing to surrender. You can't hold on to the hurt and expect to be set free. You can't cling to your pain as a form of defense and still expect healing. You will either stay hurt, or you will be free. It's your choice. God may not agree with your choice, but He will honor it. It's like being on a rollercoaster that never stops—you're trying to break free, but it's so intense that you want to jump out just to be free. If you desire liberty, the Father is offering it to you. In this season, the Lord will renew your mind and carry you to a place of health and healing.

You are not a mistake, and God is healing you in this season. He wants to free you from the guilt that keeps you replaying past experiences and feeling shameful about things you've been through or decisions you've made. Don't lose the fight. Don't let the enemy win. Take back your authority.

CLOSING PRAYER

Father God, I pray that suppression, caves, self-medication, silence, and all spirits that seek to operate in this life during this season would be cast down and placed at the feet of Jesus. I ask that the blood of Christ cleanse, restore, regenerate, and renew them with a right mind and a right spirit. As we continue, I pray that their minds be renewed according to Romans 12, that they will not be conformed to this world but transformed by the renewing of their minds. I thank you that you constantly release new information. May this new revelation continue to minister to them and serve as a guide during moments of emotional struggle. Father, I thank you for cleansing their thoughts and perceptions concerning the traumas and experiences in their lives. I thank you for showing them that their emotions are only meant to be notifications of what is operating in those moments, enabling them to reason with a clear mind and not be overwhelmed by the confusion that accompanies attacks. Father, I thank you that they will no longer desire to suppress, retreat into a cave, self-medicate, or silence themselves. Instead, they will operate from the perspective of Psalm 32:5, where David says, "I confessed all my sins to you, God, and stopped trying to hide my guilt. I said to myself, 'I will confess my rebellion to the Lord,' and you forgave me, and all my guilt was gone." Father, I thank you that our burdens are lifted, and the guilt is gone. In Jesus' name, Amen.

Emotional Me Check-In: How are you Feeling?

Find a quiet space to reflect and invite God into your time of prayer. Use the **Emotional Me Check-In** questionnaire to honestly assess your feelings, their triggers, and any Scripture that speaks to them. Release your emotions to God, seek peace, and consider any actions, like reconciliation or serving others. Reach out for support if needed, and close with gratitude.

1. What am I feeling right now? Can I name this emotion before God?

2. How would I describe this feeling in prayer to God?

3. What does the Bible say about this kind of emotion?

4. How could trusting God impact the way I respond to this emotion?

5. What step can I take to seek peace, healing, or forgiveness in relation to this feeling?

NOTES

Chapter Nine

THINK HAPPY THOUGHTS

In the last chapter, I discussed pessimism and optimism, which was a bit of a teaser for this chapter. No matter who you are, emotions are a part of everything we do in life. I've been saying this for a long time. I believe that the body of Christ, as a whole, has become so emotional that we sometimes exclude the power of God and His principles when they don't align with our carnal emotions.

The reality of our emotions is that they are here to alert us. I've said this before, but I want to keep emphasizing it, so you really catch this truth. God gave us emotions to be like alarm clocks for our feelings and thoughts. They help us define things, but they were never meant to control us. Emotions are designed to alert us to how we're feeling so we can reason through those feelings and make wise decisions, not to keep us stagnant in them. It's like the experience of pain—it's meant to teach and mature us, not box us into darkness. Pain shouldn't cause us to shut down, but rather, it should reveal the truth about what we're feeling in the moment. This allows us to properly process those emotions and let them out of our system.

As we explore various aspects of emotions, I believe this topic is especially important. I kind of work backwards, if you will. It's like how a movie is produced first, and then a prequel is made later. After the first movie, the prequel fills in the backstory. Similarly, this chapter will serve as the foundation for everything we do.

The Bible says in Hebrews 11:1, "Faith is the substance of things hoped for, the evidence of things not seen." Even in the emotional realm, there comes a point where our emotions must be guided by faith. James tells us that without faith, it is impossible to please God. This emotional phase must have a foundation, because God is the Creator of all things, including our emotions.

Opening Prayer

Father God, I thank You for what You are doing in this chapter. I thank You that someone's mind will be renewed. In Romans 12:2, You spoke through the Apostle Paul, saying, "Do not be conformed to this world, but be transformed by the renewing of your mind." Father, we know that our minds are transformed as we receive new information. Our minds are renewed as we receive new understanding.

So, Father, I pray for an impartation of new information that will bring about a renewed mind, leading to transformation in the hearts and minds of believers. I thank You, Father, that when it comes to the emotional realm, You have given us these emotions, but the enemy tries to use them against us.

As Your Word says, we should not be ignorant of the enemy's devices. There is a measure of revelation that reveals the enemy's tactics, and I pray that every believer may clearly recognize the enemy's attacks on their lives and resist him, knowing that he must flee when we resist.

So, Father, I ask that You your word will spark a resistance to the attacks of the enemy in the hearts of those reading this book. In Jesus' name, Amen.

Let's journey to Luke 8:49-56. We must reach a place where we receive the Lord to such a degree that we don't lose faith, we don't lose hope, we stop fainting, and we start growing. We must get to the point where we truly believe God. Let's look at verses 49-50 because I want to lay a quick foundation. Luke 8:49-50 says, "While he was still speaking to her, a messenger arrived from the home of Jairus, the leader of the synagogue. He told him, 'Your daughter is dead. There is no use troubling the teacher now' (The teacher being Jesus). But when Jesus heard what had happened, he said to Jairus, 'Don't be afraid; just have faith, and she will be healed.' When they arrived at the house, Jesus wouldn't let anyone go in with him except Peter, John, and James."

Sometimes, all you need is a few faith-filled people who share the same level of belief to stand with you in the room. You can't invite everyone into your space when you're praying and doing God's work, especially if they don't have the same level of faith as you. Sometimes, you must leave the faithless people out of the room, out of the conversation, and out of your journey. They don't have the capacity to believe the way God is calling you to believe. Jesus took Peter, John, James, and the little girl's parents into the house. The house was filled with people weeping and wailing, but he said, "Stop the weeping; she isn't dead. She's only asleep." Jesus is telling us to stop weeping and change our perception. Look at your situation through godly and kingdom lenses. Look at it through the lens of your faith.

Verse 55 says, "She isn't dead, she's only asleep." But the crowd laughed at him because they all knew she had died. Then Jesus took her by the hand and said in a loud voice, "My child, get up." At that moment, her life returned, and she immediately stood up. Then Jesus told them to give her something to eat. Her parents were overwhelmed, but Jesus insisted that they not tell anyone what had happened.

This is powerful because sometimes you just can't share everything God is doing for you. Not everyone has the capacity to understand. They may cause you to walk in disbelief or fall into sin. Their conversations about warfare and bad experiences may discourage you. They'll cause you to listen to their carnal minds and ruin your day with their struggles in faith. Sometimes, the warfare is so intense that it seems more important than the victory, especially when you've been beaten down.

When nothing seems possible, or nothing seems to go right, sometimes you must choose to think happy thoughts. The word "faith" means to have a formula in the mind, deciding by reasoning, reflection, or pondering, expecting hope. Faith is closely tied to reasoning and expectation. It involves deciding based on reasoning, pondering, and, most definitely, hope. Believe in happy thoughts, reason with happy thoughts, reflect on happy thoughts, and ponder happy thoughts.

The word "happy" is defined as feeling, showing, or expressing joy, pleased, characterized by or indicative of pleasure, contentment, or joy. Nehemiah 8:10 says, "Don't be dejected and sad, for the joy of the Lord is your strength." Find strength in the Lord. Find your strength in moments with God. Reason, ponder, and reflect, yet expect hope and walk in joy because in the Lord lies your strength. He's your God, your Father, your Savior, your Redeemer, and your Provider. When you can be glad about God, He'll give you strength.

> **God has not called you to weep over things out of your control.**

Philippians 4:11 says, "Not that I was ever in need. For I have learned how to be content with whatever I have." You must learn to be content. You must learn to process, ponder, and reflect on things, yet still hope in God. Draw strength from your joy because there, you will find the strength to be content. Jesus was telling Jairus, "Don't lose hope. She's not dead. Stop weeping. Stop allowing your mind to respond to the natural emotion called fear." In a house full of depression and sadness, when you have the Savior with you, stop weeping. She's not dead; she's only asleep. Change your perception. What you call death, God calls a nap.

Everything you think is dead in your life like the chance for marriage, the right job, finances, a house, a car, stop weeping. The Savior is here with you. That situation is not dead; it just hasn't come to pass yet. He hasn't forgotten about you. What you thought was a death sentence was actually the beginning of a resurrection. What you thought was a murder was a manifestation. God says change your perception of life.

God has not called you to weep over things out of your control. Get out of your emotions. Stop weeping over spilled milk and fight. Stop weeping over relationships that only God can heal. Stop weeping. Just like in verse 53, ignorant and faithless people will continue to talk about the warfare. It's not enough for them to know that they serve the God of victory. They will remain pessimistic when God walks on the scene. But God says, "She's not dead; she's only asleep."

Get to the place where you stop viewing your situation as a funeral and start seeing it as a birth. If you can get to the place of freedom, you can trust God even when it doesn't look like He's present.

The topic is not a question it's a command: think happy thoughts. Ponder on the joy of the Lord so you can find strength in your situation. It's amazing how well we quote cliches but never truly believe them: "I'm the head and not the tail, above and not beneath." Then, when all hell breaks loose, we're having panic attacks. You may desire to speak God's words every day, but His presence isn't evident in your life. Even the messenger said, "There's no use troubling the rabbi now." It's amazing how people will focus on what they see naturally, not spiritually.

As I grow deeper in my walk with Christ, I've learned to stop sharing with those who don't understand the depth of my journey. Sometimes we genuinely want to have a conversation, but we forget the people we're talking to don't have the faith to speak life. I've learned to silence myself, to stop sharing with people who speak death instead of life. When they said, "Your daughter is dead," they were declaring the death of dreams, relationships, prosperity, and more. Yet, we often allow people to speak such negativity into our lives, even though we are meant to represent the Kingdom.

People will tell you to stop troubling God. They'll try to shift your perspective, weaken your faith, and before long, you may start to doubt internally. You profess, decree, and declare over your situation, yet forget who is with you. When, as believers, will we not only know the Word but truly apply it in our lives? Jesus only allowed Peter, John, and James into the house. You need people who are anointed and know how to pray. I remind our church often: when sending a message in our group, don't ask for prayer if you've given up. Ask for reinforcements, not because you've quit, but because you're seeking victory. Two cannot walk together unless they are in agreement. Where two or more are in agreement in His name, He will be in the midst. I can't come into agreement with someone who has given up and expect to see a divine manifestation.

Many of you have been praying and seeking others to pray for you, yet you've already given up, seeing no manifestation. You've given up on yourself because the situation seems dead. No one can agree with you when you've quit. No one can intercede for you when you've quit. It's like casting pearls before swine people will take your time, your energy, your anointing, and your assignment and trample all over it. To see a breakthrough, you have to stand firm in your faith and press forward, not in resignation but with expectation of what God can do.

You must get to the place where your relationship with God is so important that you won't trample on your own situation. You must care enough about God to align with Him and sit at His table. Jesus took three mature believers with Him: Peter, His first disciple, who had experienced much with God; John; and James. Stop taking people into prayer who don't even understand the basics. Surround yourself with those who are anointed and know how to pray. Don't call them your prayer partners if they stay in disbelief.

Think happy thoughts. You can't pray for me if you're struggling with the foundations of prayer. If you're praying for me, are you also praying for yourself? Pessimism is the tendency to focus on the negative or expect the worst. Don't let that mindset define you.

You're so negative, even when you get a promotion, because you don't like the new boss. God calls you to walk into a new realm of prosperity, but all you can focus on is the fact that you now have a boss you don't really like. You've found the most negative thing to think about.

I had to change my perspective on trucking because I used to drive across the country, and I got sick and tired of it. Then, I realized those were some of the most powerful moments I had with God. I experienced more in the truck than in some churches I've been to because I changed my view. God said to me, "I know you're tired of driving from Dallas to Boston and from Dallas to Seattle, but you like the quality time we get to spend together. You talk to me, and I talk right back to you throughout the whole journey. You've built an intimate relationship with me—24 hours a day, three weeks on the road, just me and you. Why do you hate this consecrated time with me? You keep seeing it as a job, but I've always seen it as a lifestyle of consecration. It's just me and you. Why are you complaining about spending time with me?"

So, every time someone asked me how I liked the truck, I'd say, "It's alright. I just wish I was home, but God is faithful." But I wasn't showing that just minutes ago. Either God is faithful or He's not. James says a double-minded man is unstable in all his ways (James 1:8). If you're unstable in how you view God in your career, how unstable are you in other areas of your life? Surely God was in line when He inspired James to share that principle with the body of Christ.

Pessimism—a tendency to stress—isn't godly. It's a byproduct of fear, which is the opposite of faith. Fear arises when you feel like you can't control something. Panic, anxiety, depression, and sadness are just the outward expressions of that fear. This is why Jesus said to Jairus in Mark 5:36, "Don't be afraid. Just have faith." Jesus walked into the house, where people were mourning and weeping, responding naturally to the situation. He said, "Why are you afraid? I'm here."

When you worship God in your home, do you feel His presence? I'm not talking about in church, but outside of it. The presence of God is the evidence that He is near. He inhabits the praises of His people. "Inhabits" means He comes in and reveals that He resides with you. When you feel His presence, you're experiencing God without the pastor, preacher, worship team, or deacons. God reveals Himself to you in your secret place, at work, and at home. So, why are you afraid if He's shown you that He's with you?

It's not just at the altar or through a prophetic word that God reveals Himself. Jesus said, "Don't be afraid, just have faith." He asked, "Why did you lose faith when I've shown you that I'm here?" My grandfather used to say, "When something's wrong, there's a dead cat on the line." So, what is the "dead cat" in your faith? Why are you panicking, stressing, or feeling anxious or depressed when God is right there with you?

Pessimism is defined as the belief that evil, and pain outweigh any goodness or happiness. You can look it up on freedictionary.com. A "doctrine" is a belief or principle presented for acceptance, and pessimism is a belief the enemy wants you to accept. Emotions like rage, depression, and anxiety are the outward expressions of pessimism. What is happiness? It's contentment and joy, rooted in godly principles like those in Nehemiah 8:10: "The joy of the Lord is your strength." Philippians 4:11 also says, "I have learned to be content in whatever state I am in." You can either choose to be content and operate in joy, or you can believe that evil and pain outweigh goodness and happiness.

What doctrine do you live by? Pessimism is a tactic of the enemy to separate you from belief in God. The enemy's goal is always to present a bad situation to provoke disbelief. You're only separated from God when you believe the enemy over the Father. You're separated when you allow pessimism to settle in your heart and mind.

On the other hand, optimism is defined as a tendency to expect the best possible outcome or focus on the positive aspects of a situation. That's what Paul is talking about when he says, "I have a thorn in my side, but I've learned to be content because I realize that in my weakness, He is made strong." Paul brings his thorn to God, and God replies, "My grace is sufficient for you." Paul learns that in his weakness, God's power rests upon him.

In our weakness, God is made strong. Attacks and challenges come to provoke spiritual maturity. If you respond rightly—knowing that God resides in you—then you will understand that the Holy Spirit is your confidant, pointing you back to the truth of the Father. Pessimism has no place in optimism. Optimism says, "I believe God and His word. I can rejoice in my infirmities, knowing that the power of Christ will rest upon me." So, I can rejoice even in difficult times. It's not that God fixes everything immediately, although He can, but you know in your heart that the God of all things is with you.

Jesus demonstrates optimism when He walks into the room. He shows His trust in God by telling the mourners, "Stop weeping. She isn't dead; she's only asleep." Remember, this is the same Jesus who, when He arrived at the tomb of Lazarus, prayed, "Father, I thank You that You have heard Me. I know You always hear Me, but I said this for the benefit of those standing here, that they may believe."

If you experience God in your home, that means He hears you. He heard your worship, and He came to sit with you. When you pray, it's not a monologue—it's a dialogue with God. Jesus knew that the Father heard Him and was with Him. That's why He could say, "She's not dead; she's only asleep." It was the manifestation of His prayer.

Jesus said, "My house shall be called a house of prayer." He wasn't just referring to a building. The Bible says that our bodies are the temple of the Holy Spirit. Our temple needs to be a house of prayer, a place where God will hear your words and respond because you've decided to worship Him.

Here's a true story: I made a habit of praying in tongues in my truck until I felt God's presence. And you know what? It made my day go so much better. Why? Because I invited Him to sit with me. I've had accidents in my truck, even one where it flipped over in 2010. I have a scar on my head because I refused stitches. But God was with me. I've been praying in my truck for 20 years, and I'm still here to tell you today: "Lord, I thank You that You hear me."

Jesus is trying to reveal to the people that when God is with you, your emotions need to be in check. That's why He asked about their emotional response: *"Stop weeping; why are you weeping? Why are you afraid? I am here."* Why can't you think on things above, as your Word tells you? You'll come out of denial when you speak the truth. If He is here, why is your response carnal? Why do you, as I quote, *"allow yourself to settle for pessimism?"* I'm not done yet.

The last definition of optimism is the doctrine of the ultimate triumph of good over evil. You can check that out on thefreedictionary.com. Optimism, then, is a principle in the spirit realm, where you believe God will triumph over the evil trying to operate in your life. It is a doctrinal belief—a principle that you must accept for it to fully operate in your life. You can't say, "Jehovah Jireh, my provider," and then be fearful that He won't provide. Although you may quote it in knowledge, if you embrace pessimism, you are not applying the doctrine of optimism. You need to embrace optimism, because when you believe that God is the ultimate triumph over anything evil trying to enter your life—whether it's a thought, a person, a place, or a thing—that's where optimism comes in. Optimism is the strategy.

> Whether you embrace pessimism or optimism, that's what you'll experience in your life.

This is what Jesus reveals here: optimism is an expression of faith. The weeping represents fear, while optimism, happiness, and joy are expressions of faith—of believing that, although things look bad, God will prevail. We must realize, as the Scriptures say, that "life and death are in the power of the tongue." What you say has the power to produce life or death, suicide or salvation. If you have fully embraced your salvation and the Savior, there should never be a suicidal thought in your life—whether it's natural suicide or speaking death over your circumstances. That is not of the Kingdom.

Remember, God is not the author of confusion—suicide is the byproduct of confusion. When you are confused about something to the point where you feel it would be better to die than to live, that's not from God. The enemy is the author of confusion. So, if you're having such thoughts, Proverbs 23:7 says, "For as he thinketh in his heart, so is he." Whether you embrace pessimism or optimism, that's what you'll experience in your life.

Have you ever noticed that when you allow negative people to speak negativity, you end up feeling negative for the rest of the day? That's because you allowed them to sow seeds of discord into your life, and you received it. You received it when you didn't stop them. Just like Jesus did here, I'm giving you another nugget: you must stop people from sowing those seeds. That's why Jesus only took the three disciples He could trust, along with the parents. Why? Because He knew they believed.

The evidence that you believe God is that God controls your emotions. Even when things don't look right—whether it's finances, your job, your marriage, your business, or your assignment—you must know that God is in control. He is here. Proverbs 23:7 reminds us that how you look at things and what you think about them is what they will become. If you agree with negativity or pessimism, that's what you'll see. If you agree with depression, self-condemnation, or any other negative thoughts, that's what you'll experience.

Remember, the enemy comes to steal, kill, and destroy. He uses the emotional realm to infiltrate your thought patterns, because his goal is destruction. Think of pessimism through the lens of a bully. Children commit suicide because they embrace the doctrine of pessimism—they believe nothing will ever change. They were left to themselves, believing they had no one to agree with them.

The doctrines of pessimism and optimism are legal principles that, when embraced, can either bring destruction or victory in your life. God wants you to trust Him, but you must think happy thoughts. What are happy thoughts? They are thoughts that align with God's Word, regardless of how you feel emotionally. Philippians 4:8 says, "Finally, brothers and sisters, whatever is true, whatever is noble, whatever is right, whatever is pure, whatever is lovely, whatever is admirable—if anything is excellent or praiseworthy—think about such things." This is a principle that Paul presents to the Philippian church, knowing that, despite his own thorn in the flesh, he pressed on, trusting God, and the Kingdom continued to rise. Ministry went forward, and he was made stronger. You can't allow negativity to settle in your spirit. If it has the ability to shut you down, then you'll be shut down all the time, and no one will be able to get you to commit to anything because every time something bad happens, you panic.

Luke 6:45 says, "A good person produces good things from the treasury of a good heart, and an evil person produces evil things from the treasury of an evil heart." What you say flows from what is in your heart. The word "evil" is defined as morally wrong, causing harm or injury, and spiritually immoral. It is spiritually immoral to embrace the doctrine of pessimism or any emotionalism. It leads you down a path that separates you from God, because your flesh and fear are the opposite of faith.

Luke says, "A good person produces good things." When you think on good things, you produce good things because good things come from the treasury of a good heart. David says, "Your word I have hidden in my heart that I might not sin against You" (Psalm 119:11, NKJV). When you have God in your heart, only God can come from it. Emotional me: think happy thoughts. The foundation for all these lessons is your faith in God. When you think on godly things, the foundation for emotional health and healthy emotions is your faith. Do you believe God or not?

In this passage, they laughed at Him but look at what He did. He left them in ignorance because of their disgrace, disrespect, and blasphemy in laughing at God in the flesh. You need to catch this: He left them in ignorance. Verse 56 says, "Her parents were overwhelmed, but Jesus insisted that they not tell anyone what had happened." He would not even let them fully understand that a miracle had taken place. In essence, they didn't come into the full revelation of who He was because He did it in secret. Why? Because they laughed at Him.

Don't bring people around you who laugh at God and try to get them to partner with you. If they don't truly know God and are mocking Him, you can't expect them to understand His ways. Now, you've become wise. It is my prayer that as this chapter comes to a close, your emotions are no longer places of panic, but rather become an alert system that helps you process your emotions in a healthy manner. Then, you will be able to make sound decisions.

Remember, your emotions are like the notifications on your phone that alert you when you receive a message. They serve as a system to signal how you're feeling: 'Bing,' happy; 'Bing,' sad; 'Bing,' angry. It's simple. You just have to stop trying to control God's movement in your life. Surrender it freely to Him. Stir up your faith, invite Him in daily, and rest in the assurance that He hears you and dwells with you. That will bring you peace.

Do you know how many people serve God but never tangibly experience freedom and deliverance in Him? He loves you; He hears you, and He responds to you. He sent His Son, Jesus, as a sacrifice so that you and I could live a life of emotional and spiritual maturity. He sent His Son so that we could truly live a life in Christ and embrace thoughts of joy, peace, and happy thoughts.

Closing Prayer

Father, I thank You for what You will do in the lives of those who read this book in the coming weeks. I pray that each reader becomes a catalyst, impacting everyone around them. May they carry this wisdom and insight to the ends of the earth. We need emotionally healthy believers, and I ask that as they receive this impartation, it leads to both spiritual and practical manifestations. Let this knowledge rest deeply in their hearts, equipping them to share it with others.

Thank You, Father, for doing all things well. Thank You for the healing of emotions. We declare healing in their innermost places as they commit to applying each word. Your Word tells us that we cannot only be hearers but must also be doers. I pray that they faithfully work through and apply these truths until they form lasting habits in their lives.

May this book launch a movement of emotionally healthy believers, families, marriages, ministry, and marketplace relationships. I thank You that a wildfire has been sparked, one that strengthens the church and stirs lives toward transformation. We give You all the praise, glory, and honor. In Jesus' name, Amen.

EMOTIONAL ME CHECK-IN: HOW ARE YOU FEELING?

Find a quiet space to reflect and invite God into your time of prayer. Use the **Emotional Me Check-In** questionnaire to honestly assess your feelings, their triggers, and any Scripture that speaks to them. Release your emotions to God, seek peace, and consider any actions, like reconciliation or serving others. Reach out for support if needed, and close with gratitude. Regularly use this process to grow in emotional awareness and spiritual health.

1. What am I feeling right now? Can I name this emotion before God?

2. What recent event or thought may have triggered this feeling? What's the root?

3. How would I describe this feeling in prayer to God?

4. Does this feeling draw me closer to God or create distance from Him? Why?

5. What does the Bible say about this kind of emotion?

6. Have I prayed about this feeling, asking God for guidance or comfort?

7. Is there a lesson or message God might be showing me through this emotion?

8. Am I holding on to this feeling, or am I willing to release it to God?

9. What Scripture verse comes to mind that might speak to this feeling?

10. How could trusting God impact the way I respond to this emotion?

11. Are there any unaddressed needs or desires related to this feeling that I should bring to God?

12. What step can I take to seek peace, healing, or forgiveness in relation to this feeling?

13. How can I give thanks to God, even while experiencing this emotion?

14. How can I use this emotion to serve others or bring glory to God?

15. Who can I reach out to for prayer, support, or guidance as I work through this emotion?

Disclaimer:
The **Emotional Me Check-In** is a tool for personal reflection and spiritual growth. It is a self-help resource and is not intended to replace professional counseling or pastoral guidance. If you are experiencing ongoing emotional distress, we encourage you to reach out to your pastor, a mental health professional, or a deliverance minister for support. Your well-being is important, and seeking help is a vital step toward healing and peace.

NOTES

CONTINUE YOUR JOURNEY WITH EMOTIONAL ME

Thank you for walking through this journey with me. I hope the words in this book have inspired you to explore your emotions deeply and align them with God's will. Remember, understanding the matters of the soul is not just an experience—it's a transformation.

If this book resonated with you, there's even more to discover. The original sermons that inspired *Emotional Me* are filled with deeper insights, personal stories, and divine teachings that build upon these pages.

Scan the QR code below to access the full sermon series and continue exploring how to navigate emotions through a kingdom paradigm. Let these messages be a source of continuous growth, guidance, and connection as you walk in faith.

May God continue to speak to your spirit, lead your heart, and equip you for the journey ahead.

Stay blessed and continue your journey with confidence and grace.

Made in the USA
Columbia, SC
21 November 2024